Positioned to Pivot

Empowering Strategies for Your Next Chapter

Compiled by

Sharvette Mitchell

Ayanna Smith • Crystal Jones • Dana Wilson
Erika Brooks • Jennifer Cobb • Maxine Thompson
Shabrial Henderson • Shan-Nel Simmons
Dr. Tabatha Spurlock • Dr. Valarie Harris • Vinara Mosby

Mitchell Productions, LLC

Positioned to Pivot

Paperback ISBN# 979-8-9876197-2-8
Hardback ISBN# 979-8-9876197-3-5
eBook ISBN# 979-8-9876197-4-2

Published by:
Mitchell Productions, LLC
www.Mitchell-Productions.com

Back Cover Photography
Kimie James

Anthology Editor
Chandra Sparks Splond, M.S.E.
www.chandrasparkssplond.com

Book Design by Brand It Beautifully™
www.branditbeautifully.com

Table of Contents

To the Unseen Pillars of Strength:

Behind every word in this book, there's an unsung melody played by our families. To the spouses, children, parents, siblings and friends of the twelve authors who brought these pages to life — this book is a testament to your invisible yet invincible support. Your sacrifices, encouragement, and unwavering faith in our dreams have not just shaped us but have been the very foundation upon which this journey stands. We dedicate this work to you, the true architects of our aspirations.

Introduction

Welcome to a pivotal moment—not just in this book but potentially in your life. *"Positioned to Pivot: Empowering Strategies for Your Next Chapter"* is more than a collection of stories; it's a compass for those ready to navigate the often uncertain terrain of change.

Positioning, in the context of career, life, or business, is about establishing yourself in a space where your skills, experiences, and values are not only recognized but also have the room to grow and adapt. It's like finding the right starting block in a race; it's about where you stand, how you're viewed, and the potential trajectory that lies ahead. For those contemplating a career change, life transition, or business shift, positioning is critical. It determines visibility to opportunities and the alignment with one's true purpose and potential.

Pivoting, on the other hand, is the act of turning on a point to face a new direction. In life, business, and careers, it signifies a deliberate change in strategy—a transformation that starts with a single step yet has the power to alter the entire course. Pivoting is a strategic move toward new beginnings and opportunities that align more closely

Introduction

with current aspirations, needs, and the evolving market or personal landscape.

Each chapter is a testament to the power of transformation, authored by leaders who have not only faced change but embraced it with courage and emerged with wisdom to share:

Maxine Wright Thompson, M.Div., F.H., shares a "Time to Turn the Corner," signaling the critical moments to change direction.

Erika Brooks, LPC, CSAC shares her story of "Pivoting to Success," demonstrating the business resilience that pivoting can foster.

Shabrial Henderson, LCSW narrates her journey "From Chaos to Clarity," an unscripted path that led her to entrepreneurship.

Shan-Nel D. Simmons, EA MBA takes us down "The Road of Change," mapping out the landscapes of transformation.

Crystal R. Jones, LCSW, offers "Crossroad Chronicles," imparting inner wisdom for life's uncharted territories.

Jennifer Cobb, LCSW, DBTC discusses the nuances of "Pivoting Mental Health Group Practices Ownership," a testament to adaptability in professional spaces.

Dana Wilson turns the spotlight on the "You" Turn, emphasizing the courage it takes to make a personal reversal towards fulfillment.

Vinara "VEE" Mosby defines "The Pivot's True Meaning," uncovering the profound implications behind our personal experiences.

Ayanna M. Smith explores "The Depth of Saying Yes" and how affirmative choices can shape our destiny.

Dr. Valarie Williams Harris inspires with "Unleash Your Potential," aligning pivot with passion, purpose, and potential.

Introduction

Dr. Tabatha Spurlock champions "The Ultimate Comeback—Get Back in the Game," a narrative of revival and triumph.

And finally, my chapter, "The Platform Builder," lays out how to build your personal brand in the workplace to enhance morale and take control of your career destiny.

As you delve into the pages ahead, consider this book your mentor and these stories your guides. Each narrative is a stepping stone to your own pivot, a blueprint of strategies, poised to inform your next chapter. Welcome to the threshold of your transformation.

Sharvette Mitchell
Visionary Author & Compiler
Founder & CEO of Mitchell Productions

Time To Turn the Corner
Maxine Wright Thompson, M.Div., F.H.

It was May 2008, graduation day! It was the end of seven years of undergraduate and graduate school for me. I received my master's in divinity degree that day. It was indeed an exciting and auspicious moment for me.

I turned fifty-four years old that year. I started this journey in January 2002 when I was forty-eight years old. I was moving toward completing my bachelor's degree for most of my adult life. All the stars had lined up it seemed, and the time was right. I applied to and was unanimously accepted (so I am told) into the Gateway Program at Spelman College, an all-women's college in Atlanta, Georgia. The Gateway Program is for women over the age of twenty-five who wanted to finish what they had started before life issues and matters caused them to do other things. Amazingly, there were many of us in that situation. There were at least one hundred women in the program during my time there. Someone at Spelman had the great idea to open a door for us to finally pursue and complete our degree. I continue to say thank you, Spelman College. I was extremely excited, and so was my family—my husband, my daughter (who was a sophomore at Morgan State University in Baltimore, Maryland), my mother, my sisters and brothers, and many friends who supported me. I felt then that I was now able to increase my life and to move it in the direction I thought it should be. I was ready to turn the corner.

At the time, I lived in Virginia with my husband and daughter. I made the decision to attend college in Atlanta because that is where the school I wanted to attend was. Of course, I had many discussions with my spouse about returning to school and its location. He was in agreement (so I thought/believed) with me following my dream of going to this particular school. As we approached the day of my departure, we had some friction. He displayed obvious signs of slowed-down movement in terms of helping me get ready for the move. I continued to prepare mentally and physically to start the semester. I had to make choices along the way and relied on some information from readings and other sources for encouragement.

I remembered a speaker, Ruth Schimmel, at a meeting talking about courage. She said, "Courage is making a decision and following through with it." I had already made the decision and applied to college, was accepted, and was now preparing to go there and learn. I felt hindered by some of the conversations and actions in my household, but I really wanted to go do this now. I believed if I did not do it, then I would not do it later. It was a pivotal moment because I was standing at the crossroad of going or not going. I not only wanted to but needed to. I could hear Neale Donald Walsch, author of *Conversations with God*, saying "What is best for you is best for everyone."

My heart, mind, and spirit were in agreement with this decision, so, I pressed on with my move to college. After all, this was not forever but three-and-a-half years. I had one semester of credits that was accepted from the other colleges I had attended in all the places we had lived because of my husband's career. I was ready, and going back to college would—and did—change my life!

Time To Turn the Corner

The journey was amazing, and there is a much bigger story to tell about entering college as a mature adult. It was no small feat in a myriad of ways. Going to class alongside young women who were my daughter's age was indeed challenging and rewarding. I chose to be the student and no one's mother. I was always clear that I was there to complete my education just as they were. Taking this stance helped me and my fellow students to be ourselves and get the work completed that was assigned by our professors. The professors/faculty and administration were supportive as well. Many of them offered extra help if we needed it. They did not compromise the level of excellence for the courses for any of us. We had to do the work just like the traditional students. Their support and guidance helped us all to succeed.

The administration took extra time helping us register and get the proper classes and schedules. The Gateway Program office was our hub to ask the questions in private that we needed the answer to and guided us during our entire time as students. For me, this was a godsend opportunity and a place where I could thrive as an individual and a member of the group.

As I completed my coursework and graduated from Spelman College in May 2005, I applied to and was accepted at Emory University Candler School of Theology to purse a master's in divinity degree. This was indeed an eye-opening and soul-stirring journey. Once again, it was a turning-the-corner experience. The program took three years to complete and was a phenomenal journey like no other.

My decision to attend Candler brought about other situations in my marriage. I would be in Atlanta another three years completing this program. Once again, I left conversations feeling supported and encouraged. However, that was not the case as I began to experience behavioral changes from my spouse. I asked questions and did not get answers or any understanding about what was going on. After the many changes in behavior, I knew something was wrong but not the extent of it. I was in my last year, and at the end of the next-to-the-last semester, I got served divorce papers scheduled to be delivered on Christmas Eve. The saving grace was that the county office had made a decision they would no longer serve anyone papers on Christmas Eve. I did, however, receive them early in the new year as I embarked on my last and final semester.

Finishing this program was a wonderful and magnificent accomplishment for me. My graduation day and the celebration of it all was supposed to be great. It was, although I had to deal with the trauma of divorce. Was this the rain on my parade? Yes! And the timing of it all was to stop me from completing my degree. I had a moment when I had to tell myself the truth.

Again, Neale Donald Walsch put it this way: "Tell yourself the truth. Then, tell others the truth. Then, tell others the truth about yourself. In the end just tell the truth." The truth was that as I was about to embark on a different life—the old life was over. I thought it did not have to be, but one cannot make another stay where they do not want to stay. In that moment, it was a lesson in letting go. Let go of what was and/or of what you thought it was. Let go because it is time to let go. Sometimes, emotionally, letting go takes a long time.

There was no turning back at this point. I had to turn the corner. Sometimes we go willingly, and other times, we are pushed or forced in different ways to turn the corner. If you want to, you can stay put in the same place, or you can explore the many possibilities that life offers. Being a person of faith, I asked God, *What should I do now?* Many days, I just prayed and prayed more than usual. My world was shaken, and I had to do something besides crying and crying. I also prayed and cried and cried and prayed. In my asking God what I should do, I felt a quiet nudging to just move on. After all, I'd just completed a master's degree. I was, at the moment, positioned to pivot to new and greater things. I began to see my life a little clearer each day.

Time To Turn the Corner

We cannot change what has happened, but we decide what is going to happen in our near and distant future. I began to rise and feed myself—feed my spirit—some healthy food, healthy thoughts about life. I had been an avid reader most of my adult life, long before I returned to college. One of the things I read was a poem by Portia Nelson. She called it *Autobiography in 5 Short Chapters*, where she described one aspect of life.

From time to time in my life, I have gone back to this poem. It has helped me to put life in perspective again and again. After thirty years of marriage and an effort to do more with my life, the words of this poem spoke to me. The ending in Chapter 5 is most profound. I walk down a different street. We have to take another path and see where it leads. Many times, it leads to a better, more exciting, more fulfilling life. At different times, I found myself in each of the chapters and had many realizations about myself that helped me to become my better self. Each time, it was like turning a corner and restarting myself on another journey. You must do the same.

Stop living in denial about who you really are. We all have shortcomings that we can overcome if we see and accept the truth about ourselves. Begin to know for sure that you are beautiful and wonderful and smart and amazing. God gifted each of us with many marvelous attributes for us to use and share with the world. Where you are at this moment is a place for you to ready yourself to turn the corner to something more, to something great.

One of the things I secretly thought about doing was becoming a radio talk show host. I had not mentioned this to anyone, but it was a small dream. I met a young lady in the apartment complex where I lived, and we became friends. She later attended broadcasting school and spoke with me about a school project of starting an internet radio show. Along with a classmate, she asked me if I would be interested in being a host for a show. I was very excited and joined their collaboration. I did not have any experience in radio, but I had big faith in myself, and they had faith in me also. We named the show *People in the Middle,* which aired every Tuesday at six p.m. for one hour, with a replay on Sunday afternoons at one p.m.

Our show's producer had a station that he called PHRESH (*fresh*) Radio.com. We planned and launched on a Tuesday in 2013. My job was to find guests for the show. I asked my neighbor if she would be my guest. Her response was an excited yes. My first question was, *What are you in the middle of?* She began talking and surprised me with what she had to say. She was a nurse and had wanted to be a nurse from a small child. She told me about bandaging a dog's leg and taking care of scrapes for her family and friends. She also told me about her business plan to start a car service for those who did not have transportation to doctor and/or dialysis appointments. This was a great show to start with. We also had music moments and some advertising about the station and the show. We were all proud of the beginnings of the show.

I began to just ask people I knew if they were interested in being my guest. I interviewed two male friends in their late thirties about relationships and a caterer who only made healthy, delicious food who also made special meals for children with diabetes. She also had a garden of fresh vegetables, which she used in her catering business. I interviewed a woman who had many suicides in her family who was launching a church to nurture and help those who may be thinking about suicide. She was also writing a book about her own story as a survivor who was loved to life by her husband. They raised two daughters together and were planning to share their story with others. I interviewed a new mental health therapist who was working on becoming licensed. She worked for a time at a church and spoke of the mental health needs of church members.

These interviews helped me to see what I could do. Most all the people I asked to interview were willing and happy to come on the show. I closed each show with "*We hope to be your inspiration for your motivation to move you through to your transformation."* We continued doing shows for about a year, and we have plans of doing the show again. This is just one example of what can happen when we turn the corner. We can use what we have, we can realize some of the ideas we have in our heads, and make some good changes for the life ahead.

Everything must change. Nothing and no one remains the same!

— Unknown

Fast forward a few years, and most of my life has changed. Change is inevitable for all of us. I can reflect on all that has happened and find the good in it, or I can look back and continue to grieve and replay the past. I choose to extract any good that has come from these life events. For one thing, I completed my college degree and my master's degree. Second, I am no longer in a relationship with someone who does not want to be in a relationship with me. Third, I am in a peaceful place emotionally, physically, and spiritually. Turning one corner started me down this road to change. I turned several corners over time, which has helped me to let go of what I could not hold on to anyway.

Letting go demanded additional changes that I may not have wanted to face at all, but in retrospect, I am very happy that I did. We have to stop looking at change as a bad thing and begin to see it with hope. Jerome Groopman, a medical doctor and author who wrote about hope in his book *Anatomy of Hope,* suggested that "hope is effective forecasting," looking forward to a brighter future.

We can grab on to hope in our changing times and forecast for ourselves that the bright light within us will shine on the path ahead to assist us in navigating to the greatness that is ours already. If we can do this, we would not resist change in the way that we do. I am not remiss in proclaiming that change is easy. Change is hard. Because it is hard, many of us just avoid it when we can.

Change means to alter or make different. An example of change is to have ices cubes in a glass. Let it sit at room temperature, and the ice melts and becomes water. Now the glass has water instead of ice. Change. When life turns up the temperature, something will change. It is up to us to manage that change in the best way that we can.

William Bridges, educator and author, has written a book entitled *Managing Life's Changes*, where he describes the process for us. His work examines the steps we take to becoming whole when change happens in our lives.

Life will bring many changes. Change happens to us, or we can make a change. Change can happen because of a car accident or a move, a promotion or a layoff. A literal storm comes and blows the house down or a flood or any type of trauma and we must change. We can initiate change by pursuing a new job or quitting our current one. We can decide to move across town or cross country or out of the country. However change comes, we have to deal with the consequences of it. Take some time to reflect and to process. Spend time with yourself and the divine seeking direction and guidance. Become at peace with yourself and God. Prepare as best you can and then turn the corner with hope and trust in yourself. When you turn the corner, your life will never be the same again, but will be brighter than you have ever known.

Meet the Author | Maxine Wright Thompson, M.Div., F.H.

Maxine Thompson received her master of divinity with a concentration in faith and health from Candler School of Theology at Emory University in Atlanta, Georgia, where she received many awards and accolades. She received her bachelor of arts degree from Spelman College in Atlanta, Georgia, where she was a Pauline E. Drake Scholar, Daughters of the Covenant Mentoring Program participant, and inductee into the Divine Legacy of Women in Ministry in the historic Sisters Chapel, WISDOM Center in April 2007.

She is the former director of event planning and constituent relations at the Great Bethune-Cookman University in Daytona Beach, Florida, where she was the liaison for outreach programs, which connected the church, the community, and the university. She also worked with faculty development where she presented seminars on subjects of Spirituality in the Workplace and Self Care.

Maxine combines her creative passion for lifting others through dynamic and engaging workshops to help others with self-discovery. She works with individuals and groups at retreats and special events offering sessions in change / transition / transformation, divorce /

depression/determination, and women/people in the middle of life crisis. Maxine is a lifetime encourager who seeks to remind others that you will get through your difficult time, and life's inevitable changes are the catalyst for your transformation.

Maxine also lived in the Kingdom of Saudi Arabia for ten years, affording her the opportunity to travel and explore more than forty-two countries and four continents.

Pivoting to Success
How Pivoting Has Helped My Business Survive and Thrive
Erika Brooks, LPC, CSAC

When I went to graduate school for rehabilitation counseling, I had no idea I would be a therapist. I thought that I would go to school, get my master's degree, and work as a case manager in some type of alcohol and drug treatment program. In this role, I would connect people to resources they needed for substance abuse and mental health needs. (I have learned over the years that it involves a lot more than that.) I didn't think I wanted to be a therapist because what if I said the wrong thing. What if I messed someone up? What if I couldn't help anyone? I knew that substance abuse was something that had been near and dear to my heart and that it was—and still is—a much-needed service. I also knew that I was supposed to help others in some way. I figured that with my gift of gab and love of people, I would be able to meet my clients where they were and help them achieve their goals and make the changes they needed to live their best lives. That was my plan, but little did I know how that plan would change.

On April 21, 2002, I was nearing the end of my graduate school career. I was completing my last three classes and internship. For my internship, I was an outpatient clinician at a mental health facility. This facility was small and had only three therapists, and I was studying for an important certification exam. I had been studying for weeks, and my nerves were starting to get the best of me. I knew that only the office manager was in the office, and it would be a perfect time to just sit with her and talk.

While the office manager and I were talking, a client came in wanting to talk with someone because they were facing a crisis. Being the only clinician there, I agreed to talk to them. This person was not known to me, but was known to the other therapists, and it was clear they were struggling with something. I did my best to help them figure out how to handle the situation at hand, weigh the pros and cons, and find comfort in their decision. As we finished, this person thanked me and asked if they could hug me. At this point in my career, I was not comfortable with hugging clients as I worried it may blur a boundary, but I did. Something told me that I needed to hug this person. When they left, I talked with the office manager and told her about my nerves, because remember, I thought my path in life was to be a case manager and not a therapist. I wrote my detailed notes for the person's regular counselor and left.

On the way back home, I kept wondering why this encounter happened today of all days. The day when there was no clinician staff at the office. The day when I could not reach anyone by phone (believe me, I tried several times). The day that Junior, as my site supervisor affectionately called me, decided to take a break from studying and come hang out.

On the next day of my internship, I returned to the office and met with my supervisor. He told me that he had met with the client. He asked me to explain what had happened with the client and what I did. Of course, the rookie Junior was nervous and hoping the client was okay. He also asked me how I felt I handled this and what I would have done differently. Immediately, I began thinking that I had royally messed this client's life up and I was going to fail my internship. To my surprise, my supervisor had a different view. He began to read a letter where the client praised me for my compassion, attentiveness, and caring nature. The client spoke about how scared they were of making the wrong decision and feeling empowered by our conversation. They commented that giving them a hug made me more relatable, trusting, and caring. Their last comment was that I was the best therapist to have handled that situation. My supervisor's final words to me in that meeting: "You done good, Junior."

April 21, 2002, is a day that I will always remember. I will never forget that meeting. I will never forget that client. I will never forget that feeling. After meeting with my supervisor, I realized why I was there that day. I realized why I was unable to get in touch with my supervisor. I realized why that member came in that particular day and time. It had been suggested by my supervisor and advisors that I consider becoming a therapist, but I wouldn't hear it. I had a plan. I knew the path that I was on, and I was going to do that. But that was not what was to be. Oh, but God! God had a different plan for me, and because I had not been listening to the people He sent, He sent the message another way.

If you know me, you know that I fully believe in and follow what God has for my life. Many people follow some Higher Power and have learned that our plan is not always in line with our Higher Power's plan. We have to learn to deviate from what we *thought* was going to be and follow what *is* to be. That is one of the biggest lessons I've learned about faith and following the plan. You pivot directions.

Since that day, I have learned the importance of pivoting—allowing myself to be open to change. Whether it is changing the style of technique I use, changing the direction with the care of services, or changing direction of a session, learning to pivot has helped me be successful with clients and to grow in directions I didn't think were possible.

So, What Is Pivoting, and Why Is It Important?

The word *pivot* is a French borrowing that slowly became a part of the English language. In the fourteenth century, it was a noun, designating a shaft or a pinon that something turns. Later, it was used to describe any central person or thing around which action revolves. Later in the nineteenth century, it became a verb to indicate the act of turning about a point. According to Merriam-Webster.com, *pivot* is defined as to adapt or improve by adjusting or modifying something (such as a product, service, or strategy). The example given for this definition is *"In my first product business, I didn't know when to pivot and lost everything as a result"* from India Gary-Martin.

After reading this, I began to look at pivoting as a slight turn of direction—or it can be a do-over—and how this could be a good thing. Being able to pivot also helps to increase our resilience. We are then better able to deal with setbacks and challenges if we are open to other approaches or ways to act. Being able to pivot allows us to be able to seek feedback from our customers/clients. We can use that feedback to make changes that are more customer focused and that are best for the business and the customer. Finally, being able to pivot allows us to be able to stay competitive and adapt to the market.

I will admit that I can be a creature of habit and not like change, but I have learned that it is vital as a business owner to be flexible and willing to make changes as needed. Here are some of the lessons I have learned that may be helpful to you as a business owner/leader.

Sometimes You Don't Want to Pivot, but It Is Necessary

Probably one of the biggest pivots for me and my business occurred in March 2020. I had been having individual therapy sessions in person three to four times a week. I had access to a receptionist who would alert me when my clients arrived and a lovely waiting area for them to sit in as I finished with the previous client. In March 2020, the world was hit with a pandemic, COVID-19. Immediately, the state went on lockdown, and after the lockdown was over, the majority of people did not want to leave their homes for fear of contracting this virus, which was wreaking havoc. But people still needed therapy, and I was going to help my clients.

In a matter of days, I had to begin providing telehealth services. This presented somewhat of a challenge in that I had to learn about different telehealth regulations and requirements, what telehealth platforms met the standards for HIPAA compliance, and making sure my clients were willing to participate in a new way for therapy. I also needed to make sure this was cost prohibitive and that my insurance covered telehealth.

Was this change easy? For some of my clients, it was not. They didn't like the idea of not being in person. They didn't always have privacy for their sessions. Sometimes the internet connection would fail. For me, there were some advantages, but there were some drawbacks. Yes, I felt some loss in picking up some cues, but it was convenient and it was safe. I told the client that sometimes the pivot is not your change or your desire but necessary. We were under a mandatory shutdown and could not meet in person. Going out could have been detrimental to some of my members as well as myself. This pivot was necessary because not having the services was not an option.

Having to make this change helped me to realize that not all members will be able to come in for face-to-face and that having an option of telehealth is ideal. It also helped me to realize that I was missing a part of the audience who may have mobility or transportation issues. Having the telehealth services opened me up to more clients.

Take Advantage of the Time Pivoting May "Cost You"

As I stated earlier, being a therapist was not my initial plan for my career. I accepted that my calling was to help others, but my plans were slightly altered. After April 21, 2002, I turned my direction toward therapy. I started taking steps to complete the process to be licensed in order to do this. This was not always an easy road. There were bumps, such as the work I had done for one year after graduation did not count toward licensure because of a small technicality. I had to redo that time with another place and another supervisor. Thankfully, I was able to do this at a new place of employment.

Although this felt like a setback and wasted time, this proved to be beneficial. This time was important as I learned to step out of my comfort zone. With this new employment, I was working with a different population than I had expected to work with. This was a temporary job working with people in psychiatric emergencies. Although I had knowledge of working with mental health, counseling, and understanding of crisis, I had never really worked with this population.

This new opportunity afforded me the chance to learn about a new aspect of mental health. If I had not left the previous job, I would have continued to work with the population I was comfortable with and had always known. I would not have the direct work with serious mental illness or the geriatric population. I would have pigeonholed myself in my career. I also continued to sharpen my skills as well as build a reputation as a clinical professional.

I used this time to begin to feel more comfortable in my skills and to believe I indeed could be a solid therapist. I built relationships with others in my field who helped me to hone my skills, as well as to understand that I will not always know the right thing to say or do. I accepted the mentoring and training others wanted to give me. I asked question after question. Since I had to carry a small caseload of clients, I practiced different theories and techniques. I figured out what worked well for me and what didn't. I began to develop my style and comfort zone.

In time, I began to feel more confident in my therapeutic technique. I realized the more confident I felt, the more at ease my clients were with talking to me. I also realized they were reporting that they felt they were making progress. In hindsight, I am thankful that I did extra hours because I learned more about the profession, opportunities within the profession, and honed my skills. I also developed a network of colleagues who were willing to refer clients to me when I was ready to start my own business.

Be Willing to Gain New Ideas for Products and Services

I have been successful in working with clients and their mental health concerns. It has been a very rewarding but sometimes challenging job. As I have worked with clients, I have continued to educate myself on how best to care for my clients and different techniques. As I studied and worked, I listened to my clients on what else could be helpful in their journeys. I realized that "talk therapy" may not be the only avenue to assist them. I learned to use aromatherapy with members who may be stressed. I began teaching my clients how to use journaling when they felt they could not use their voice. I began to use affirmations with my clients when they struggled with self-esteem. These small changes have led to new ideas and creations of different products for members. For me, having products is a way to increase visibility, another stream of income, and another way to help members. They are able to use products, such as affirmation cards or journals, to continue the work they are doing in session.

From listening to people in my target audience (those I like working with), there is often more than one person who is needing to hear the same information someone else needs. This led me to developing and marketing webinars and speaking engagements, which are great in the sense that you can reach more than one person at a time. It is another stream of income. It also can be done virtually or in-person. I have been able to tailor the presentation to meet the needs of the audience and address whatever concerns/questions they may have. I had some reluctance about speaking engagements, but I have enjoyed meeting new people, having lively discussions, and being challenged to come up with more topics. I have also received referrals for other speaking engagements or work from speaking engagements.

I also cannot leave out being willing to learn where your target audience is and spending a little more time there. For example, I know that I enjoy working with African-American females, roughly twenty-five to forty. I would post information on social media, but looking at the data, I was missing this age group. I created a survey and found that most of them were using TikTok and Instagram versus Facebook. This has prompted me to pay attention to those outlets versus things such as Twitter, as they are not there.

The survey also told me that they are more into audio media such as podcasts. This has helped me tailor to meet my members' needs and decrease some work on myself. This will also help you to stay on top of what is important to your target audience and give them what they need, which will keep them coming back to you for services.

Take the Time to Grow

Over the years, I have had a lull in clients. Sometimes it was due to the season—the beginning of summer is the time I experience more no-show appointments. Sometimes, it is due to the economy (the beginning of the year is a little lighter than other times). There are also times when my client load rises, such as during COVID-19, the beginning of a school year, and holidays. Whenever there are spikes in either direction, I take a step back and review what is going on. I pay attention to if there is a trend. In taking a step back, I've learned what days and times are best to schedule appointments. I also researched and found a better way to remind clients of appointments and meetings. This has decreased no shows and also increased my productivity.

Understanding the importance of pivoting is a true value to individuals and business owners. It helps us to adapt, learn, continue growing, and stay current in this ever-changing world. Being able to pivot will help you make better decisions, decrease risks, and stay relevant in your chosen business field.

Erika Brooks, LPC, CSAC

Meet the Author | Erika Brooks, LPC, CSAC

Erika Brooks, LPC, CSAC, is a licensed professional counselor and a certified substance abuse counselor in the state of Virginia. She received her master of science in rehabilitation counseling from Virginia Commonwealth University. She is the owner of Enlightenment Counseling Services, LLC. Erika enjoys working with women's health issues, including mental health issues, self-care, and trauma and grief therapy. She has been a guest on several podcasts to discuss topics around mental health and self-care, particularly in the African-American community. She is a co-author of *PEARLS: Wisdom and Advice for Emerging Leaders*. Erika is a contributing editor to *Hope for Women* magazine. She is active in her church and in her community and is a member of National Coalition of 100 Black Women. In her spare time, she enjoys time with her family and friends, reading, and taking care of herself. Contact her at brookslpc@gmail.com.

From Chaos to Clarity
My Unscripted Route to Entrepreneurship
Shabrial Henderson, LCSW

Boss: Hey, Shabrial, can I talk to you in my office?

Me: Sure.

Boss: As you know, we have been restructuring the company, and after consideration, we have decided to eliminate your position.

Me: Okay. Thanks. When is my last day?

Boss: Friday, but we will continue your payroll over the next two weeks.

Me: Okay. Thanks.

Confused? Let's unpack that.

As a clinical social worker with more than six years of expertise in the mental health field, hearing that my position was getting cut was shocking. Like, what? Clinicians are the backbone of mental health services. And I'm not gonna lie, I was salty. But not because I was losing my job—I was upset because I didn't quit first. I was already plotting my exit strategy; I hadn't pulled the trigger yet.

Funny how life works. I was starting to get too comfortable in the dysfunction and had been distracted from working on my dream. But now, since being fired, I suddenly had the freedom to diligently work on launching my private practice and to start a new journey to entrepreneurship.

Now that you know my turning point, let's rewind.

In May 2018, I was fresh out of graduate school and excited for two reasons: I didn't have to write another discussion post or ten-page paper, and I could finally get my life started like a "real" adult instead of being in limbo like I have been for the past seven years. Yes, I said seven years. Don't judge. I changed my major twice while an undergraduate and stayed an extra year. Anyway, I was heavy on the job search, which was tedious and frustrating because the number of interview requests didn't align with the number of applications I submitted.

A few months later, in August 2018, I secured an entry-level district school social worker position in a rural county. I was excited; I started the school year with minimal expectations and an eagerness to learn.

Within the first year, I adapted to the role and was offered a permanent position. Over the next two years, I continued to excel in this role, which led me to start my residency as a licensed clinical social worker.

Shortly after my residency started, I was experiencing burnout. I was providing social work services across an entire district, which consisted of four schools, and I needed help because ya girl was overwhelmed. Because I was spread so thin, I wasn't gaining the necessary clinical hours for my residency. After three years, I decided it was time for a change. At the end of 2020, I started a new position as a resident therapist, and I loved it. I felt like face-to-face interaction with clients was exactly what I needed to enhance my clinical knowledge and experience.

From Chaos to Clarity

It wasn't until 2021 that I decided I wanted to go full-time, but not without a plan. Building and sustaining a full-time caseload couldn't be too hard since I could maintain a consistent caseload within the first few months, so I scheduled a meeting with my regional director to learn the logistics of this full-time transition and assess how realistic it was.

Let's say this is when things took a turn. Y'all, I was sold a dream! Ultimately, building a caseload took longer than initially four to six weeks. At first, I was comfortable with a slow build-up because I had a small nest egg saved to cover my expenses; however, it didn't last very long. While I enjoyed working with clients and witnessing their progress, it was a mess administratively. There was an overhaul of billing concerns, ethical issues, scheduling conflicts, and financial instability.

One thing I don't play with is my money, and let's be honest, it doesn't matter how much you enjoy what you do, everyone wants to get paid and have a sense of stability. Fast forward to six months later, I was frustrated with the continuous client cancellations, poor insurance verification, lack of support from management, unrealistic scheduling expectations, software changes, corporate changes, and most importantly, financial instability. After experiencing all of this, I stayed. Why, you may ask? Because I was receiving free supervision and only had a couple hours left. I didn't want to lapse in finding a new supervisor, notifying the board, waiting for approval, and resuming residency. At the time, it made more sense to wait until I completed my supervision hours and then quit. After completing my clinical hours, I was fed up and decided to leave earlier than expected due to this incident.

At the time, a client was charged nine hundred dollars for the past three months of therapy sessions without warning. They were, rightfully so, feeling betrayed and frustrated, and I felt their pain; I was upset on their behalf because I was their therapist, and this shouldn't have happened, and I didn't want the client to judge me. Unbeknownst to me, the company underwent a corporate freeze on all copayments and later backdated all payments at one time, which was why this client owed this amount.

I apologized profusely and promised to sort it out with the billing department. After speaking with the billing department, I thought, *I'm tired of all these careless mistakes. This isn't the first person I have had to advocate for, and no one should have to go through this constantly.*

I contemplated the idea of starting my private practice, but this experience ignited my passion. If I started my practice, I thought I could handle these situations more swiftly and avoid these mistakes. Who would have thought that frustration would be all the spark needed to consider full-time entrepreneurship? But let me tell you, learning to pivot during this journey isn't for the faint-hearted.

From Employee to Employer

In March 2022, I received my approval email from the board to take my LCSW (Licensed Clinical Social Worker) exam. While I was excited, I wasn't prepared. Initially, I started studying for my exam but fell off track a month prior due to life happening. A few weeks after my approval, I started a new role as a clinical supervisor. This role was ideal as I heavily contemplated entrepreneurship but lacked managerial experience. I thought this new role would perfectly balance people and business management. On my first day on the job, I arrived at work, and no one (literally no one) was there. I sat in my car for one hour before the office manager came. Despite an apology from the office manager, I was frustrated, but I maintained my composure as I didn't want to give off a "bad" first impression. Over the next few weeks, I decided not to make long-term plans with this company. I observed several issues that didn't align with my professional values. It motivated me to start taking baby steps toward launching my business.

I started noticing a pattern, and being frustrated motivated me to change, so I got serious about studying for my LCSW exam and created an action plan. On the test day, I failed by three points and was disappointed, not because I couldn't retake it but because I couldn't make my exit as planned. After giving myself time to grieve, which lasted about twenty-four hours, I appealed and rescheduled for the following month. As my next test date approached, I panicked, afraid of failing again, I pushed off the test date for another month. But if I'm being honest, I only panicked because I hadn't been studying consistently like the first time. It was time to refocus and not allow my anxious thoughts to win, which they didn't because on my next test date, I passed and was officially an LCSW.

I jumped into overdrive after passing my exam. I was consumed with weeks of research preparing for the business launch. Let me tell you, launching a business isn't just about having a vision and a passion for helping people—it's about getting into the nitty-gritty details. We're talking about state, federal, and county requirements, tax filing, insurance credentialing, liability insurance, website development, branding, and marketing strategies.

I remember sitting at my desk, buried under stacks of papers, thinking, *I'm just one person. How in the world am I going to juggle all this?* The feeling was overwhelming. Where would the money come from to support all these activities? Remember that job I was eager to leave? Well, I had to stay longer to offset these startup costs. Things were starting to align. I had scheduled a professional photo shoot, completed the company logo, the website was in development, and my listing for a popular therapist directory was complete. Reflecting, I felt confident my plans aligned, and then I got fired.

Having a side hustle is essential in the mental health field. Over the years, I witnessed high turnover, so I knew to stay prepared, so financially I was okay. Being fired around the holidays and attempting to launch a business wasn't the initial plan. I didn't want to make a rash decision and forcefully launch because things weren't solidified, and this business represents me. Instead, I launched my directory two months in advance to test my target audience and make changes as needed. After the directory launch, I secured two clients before my official launch date. Within the first two months of business, I went from two to fifteen clients.

When Imposter Syndrome Strikes

Now that we've discussed my journey to entrepreneurship, let's discuss another hurdle I faced: imposter syndrome. Have you ever felt like you're not "good enough" to start a business or take that leadership role? Welcome to the club. You're not the only one. Imposter syndrome is that nagging sensation of self-doubt, that inner critic whispering that you're a "fraud" and that someone will find you out despite all your accomplishments.

Confession time: I faced my own bouts of imposter syndrome, even after years of rigorous education and training. I remember the anxiety I felt leading up to my launch date. I didn't want to celebrate it with anyone. I wanted my website to go live and see what happened. This is why it is essential to have a support system. My close friends urged me to have a launch party to celebrate this major accomplishment. Though they were right, I struggled with the thoughts that raced through my mind: *Can I really do this? Am I prepared enough? What if they don't like my website? I hope this sounds genuine and not like a sales pitch.*

You see, I've always been a humble person. I enjoy being behind the scenes, but sometimes you've got to step into the spotlight, whether you feel ready or not. But then it hit me: Why not celebrate this significant milestone in my life? I had worked hard, I had the qualifications, and I was offering something of genuine value to my clients. I also knew deep down that if I let imposter syndrome hold me back, I'd miss out on success and the opportunity to make a meaningful impact in people's lives.

So, I silenced that inner critic and threw that launch party, and you know what? It was a hit. My friends and colleagues came, and their support was a real boost. More importantly, it was a reminder that I deserved to be celebrated, not just as a clinician, but as a business owner and as a person who had taken the bold step to follow her dreams.

The Art of Pivoting

If there's anything I've learned on this journey, the art of pivoting is crucial. Whether it's from school to the workforce, from employee to employer, or from doubting yourself to empowering yourself, knowing how to pivot can make all the difference. You see, life will throw curveballs. How you handle them is the real test.

For me, those curveballs often acted as wake-up calls, steering me away from situations that were no longer serving me and toward opportunities that I would never have considered otherwise. When I got fired, it forced me out of my comfort zone, made me confront my fears head-on, and ultimately guided me toward the path that I'm on now—a path that aligns with my core values, expertise, and the real impact I can make in my clients' lives.

In the grand scheme of things, I see every setback as a setup for a comeback. When I felt burnout creeping in at my previous job, it was a signal that I needed to pivot toward something more sustainable, which turned out to be entrepreneurship. When I faced imposter syndrome, it was a sign that I was stepping into new, uncomfortable territory, which is almost always where growth happens.

Here's What You Can Do

If you are currently contemplating pivoting and are uncertain how to strategize your next move, here are a few things to consider:

- **Self-check:** Take a moment to evaluate your situation. Are you happy? Are you learning? Are you growing? If not, it might be time for a pivot.
- **Dream Big but Start Small:** Think about what you want to achieve, break it down into smaller, actionable steps, and start working on them.
- **Be Your Own Advocate:** If you don't advocate for yourself, who will? Don't be afraid to put yourself out there, to celebrate your successes, and to ask for what you need.
- **Silence the Inner Critic:** Recognize when imposter syndrome kicks in and counteract it with positive affirmations, and if possible, get a hype crew—friends and loved ones who remind you of your worth.
- **Stay Prepared:** Always have a plan B, especially in fields like ours where the turnover can be high.

Embracing Flexibility

The one consistent thing in life is change, without a doubt. Whether you're an emerging entrepreneur or a seasoned pro, you'll find that being adaptable is invaluable. I realized this first-hand when establishing my virtual therapy practice. You'll draft a business plan, set target dates, and outline objectives, but when you think you've cracked the code, life throws you a curveball.

Flexibility isn't merely an ability to adapt; it's about anticipating and welcoming change. Consider it a form of yoga for your decision-making processes—it might stretch you, but it also fortifies your resilience.

So, you know how in yoga, you're encouraged to find your edge—that point where it's uncomfortable but not painful? It's all about pushing boundaries to create growth. This is no different when discussing flexibility in decision-making and embracing risks, especially as a business owner.

First off, let's tackle the anticipation piece. Now, if you've been adulting for a minute, you've seen how quickly things can change—markets fluctuate, pandemics happen, and TikTok trends vanish overnight. So being on your toes ready to pivot isn't just brilliant; it's survival. Anticipating change isn't about having a crystal ball. It's about looking at your field and asking what's next. It's akin to looking at the weather forecast before stepping out; you might still get caught in the rain, but at least you've got an umbrella handy.

And then comes the "welcoming change" part. Many people see change and react like they touched a hot stove—pure recoil. But change is inevitable. It's like those endless updates to your phone's operating system: You can ignore them for a while, but eventually, you will have to hit Update to keep things running smoothly. Welcoming change is less about loving what it represents and more about embracing growth and new possibilities that come with it.

It's like this: I had doubts when I decided only to provide virtual services. Would the experience be less "real" for my clients? Would the intimacy be lost in translation? But guess what? Taking that risk not only expanded my reach but also equipped me with tools and experiences that I could never have gained otherwise. That's the resilience part—being stretched but coming back stronger.

Building a Strong Support Network

Success is never a solo act. From personal experience, I know that having a solid support network isn't just beneficial; it's indispensable. The worth of these connections—be it friends for emotional support, mentors for wisdom, or peers for unique viewpoints—cannot be overstated.

Case in point: Selecting a name for my business was daunting. My close friends' perspectives were pivotal in gauging how prospective clients would respond.

So, how do you cultivate such a vital network? First, be supportive of yourself. It's a reciprocal relationship. Next, seek individuals who embody your aspirations. Remain open to advice, initiate rich conversations, and above all, be someone others can depend on.

Wrapping Up

I'll leave you with one of my favorite quotes by Marianne Williamson: *Our deepest fear is not that we are inadequate. Our deepest fear is that we are powerful beyond measure... Who are you not to be brilliant, gorgeous, talented, fabulous?*

What scares us isn't the idea that we're not good enough; it's the realization that we could be extraordinary. Why hold back from being a shining star in your life—talented, unique, and fabulous?

You see, fear and doubt are like that friend who shows up uninvited, eats all your snacks, and crashes on your couch. You didn't ask for them, but there they are, and now you've got to figure out what to do with them. It's natural to feel apprehensive when you're about to make a major life move or pivot.

But here's the kicker: Fear can be a roadblock or a stepping stone. You choose. What's vital here is believing in your abilities and acknowledging your value. Remember, you have a unique narrative; your experiences and insights matter. If you're feeling like you're on the edge of something great, but fear is holding you back, consider this your sign to leap. Don't let fear rob you of your brilliance. You are, and always have been, powerful beyond measure. It's about time you embraced it.

Meet the Author | Shabrial Henderson, LCSW

Shabrial Henderson, LCSW, is a licensed clinical social worker in the state of Virginia. A proud alumna of Virginia Commonwealth University, she holds a master's degree in clinical social work. As the founder and owner of New Insight Clinical Counseling, LLC, Shabrial operates a virtual private practice based in the heart of Virginia.

Specializing in working with millennial men and women, she addresses challenges ranging from depression and anxiety to relationship issues and life transitions. Guided by a deep understanding of the pressures of societal expectations and the transformative power of overcoming barriers, Shabrial is highly committed to each client's unique journey. This ethos is encapsulated in her co-authored book, Positioned to Pivot: Empowering Strategies for Your Next Chapter, which highlights her dedication to empowering individuals to tackle life's changes with strategic insight and confidence.

But her influence doesn't stop at the therapist's door. Shabrial is also an eloquent speaker and event host, focusing on critical mental health and wellness topics. Known for her engaging style, she excels at distilling complex subjects into relatable, digestible insights that resonate with diverse audiences.

Outside the professional sphere, Shabrial is a globetrotter at heart. Her love for exploring new destinations enriches her life and informs her holistic approach to mental health care.

For more information, contact her at admin@newinsightclinical-counseling.com or www.newinsightcc.com.

The Road of Change
Shan-Nel D. Simmons, EA MBA

How do you change your strategy while maintaining your vision and your purpose? What is required to tear down everything you've built thus far to then rebuild it again using a new direction that is bigger, grander, or even astronomical in its potential impact?

Whether in business or your personal life, one comes to a crossroads where you can either continue doing what you have always done and be okay with that, or you can take the other path—the path where if you are willing to make the shift and live your dreams in real life you will exceed your own definition of success. The other path is the road of change.

At seven years of full-time entrepreneurship as of 2023, I stood at that crossroads for my business and for my life, and I am taking my first steps onto the road of change.

Let me share some wisdom I found from the book of Philippians in the Bible. In Philippians 4:11–13 NIV, the apostle Paul writes, "I am not saying this because I am in need, for I have learned to be content whatever the circumstances. I know what it is to be in need, and I know what it is to have plenty. I have learned the secret of being content in any and every situation, whether well fed or hungry, whether living in plenty or in want. I can do all this through Christ who gives me strength."

These insightful verses have served me as a valuable guide for navigating how to shift onto the road of change while protecting the integrity of my purpose and vision. Here are some of the epiphanies I've experienced so far through my own season of shifting and changing I would like to share with you as a motivation, an education, and support.

Embrace Change

Life changes, and so do plans, and that is okay. Change is included in the design of life, which is why there are seasonal weather changes throughout the year and why people age from infants to elders.

Change is natural and inevitable. It does not have to be negative, and it is usually the spark of growth and improvement. Even with the best of plans, some circumstances will require you to shift gears and adjust your approach.

But plans can change without outside circumstances. Being content with your choice to change your mind is one of the best graces you can grant yourself. You are not ungrateful for what you currently have by wanting more or wanting something different for your life. Therefore, whether you are living in a time of want or living in a time of having plenty, change should be received as a part of your journey.

Adapt a Guiding Principle

To determine if your vision and your purpose should remain the same after you decide it is time to change your approach, you must revisit some fundamental truths about yourself. Here is a list of a few suggested questions to consider what your fundamental truths are:

- Who are you?
- What do you want to achieve?
- How do you want to be remembered?
- What drives you to keep going?
- What is success for you?
- How will you know you've reached your own level of success?

Notice I did not say what is your why. I intentionally asked who, I asked what, and I asked how questions. Although change happens, why we do something fluctuates more often than who we are, what we are doing, and how we are going to do it in our business and in our life.

Whenever I want to further illustrate this point, I share the scene from the movie *Black Panther* when the late Chadwick Boseman's character T'Challa was almost defeated by M'Baku (Winston Duke), and I highlight how T'Challa's mother (Angela Bassett) did not stand up to yell "Show them your why!" No, no, no. She yelled, "Show them who you are!"

Who you are now is a better compass of how you will navigate changes and challenges in your life as they arise than your why of the moment. Who you are cements your vision and purpose, which will remain throughout and after the change in any and every circumstance. It is crucial to establish your North Star to maintain a clear sense of your direction as you explore what is changing for you within this season of your business and your life. That is why it is important to be clear of who you are, what you believe, and what matters most to you during times of change. Stay true to yourself.

Release Comfortable Crutches

I learned during my season of change that although there are parts of me that I will honor and incorporate in all I do until the end of time, I am introspective and reflective enough to know when some methods I used in the past no longer serve my vision or my purpose so I must consider letting them go. While I can clearly see how older strategies hinder my steps on my road of change, the challenge I faced of letting go of my old ways meant I must release something I was used to doing that had become familiar, cozy, and comfortable. Can you relate?

This is not about confidence—or lack of it—or fear of making a move. This is about being set in a routine that served you well when it was relevant to your vision and your purpose. You are aware that routine no longer holds a place in the plans for where you are going, but you like what you like.

You have become set in your ways, but what you did not realize is you allowed what is comfortable about your old ways to become a crutch by not letting go, and your old ways are slowing down your steps as you progress down the road of change.

We—because I am guilty of this as well—must let go of the comfortable crutches. We must stand tall on the strength of our faith in ourselves and the belief that the changes happening will work if we fully welcome these new approaches and plans into our businesses and lives as we transition and transform into our new normal.

When your plans are aligned with the higher purpose of your vision, your purpose, and your faith, you will begin to draw divine strength and know you have the resilience and perseverance to do all things. Let the comfortable crutches go.

Focused and Flexible

Change requires you to learn a dance between holding fast to what must remain the same but also knowing when to allow space for something different and new to enter at any moment. Sometimes, a roadmap, a course, a coach, or a book might be able to give you the steps you need to know the perfect balance between what is aligned with your vision and what is a required adjustment to keep moving forward.

But many times, you will have to trust in your own ability to decide for your own purpose and your own vision what is the right next step for you because that is truly what it means when they say being a leader is risky. There is no right and there is no wrong decision when you are deciding from your own vision. Sometimes, the decision will lead you to a place of having less than what you desired, and sometimes, the decision will go exceedingly better than you could have ever dreamed.

The attitude you must acquire is that you will be satisfied with what happens regardless of the outcome as long as your actions are based on your vision and your purpose. That is the secret.

If it worked out, you are satisfied to see the reward of a plan well executed. But if the results reveal things not going as planned, you should still be satisfied for the following reasons:

1. You made your vision a reality. Many other people allow plans to live and die in their heads while you made your plans happen.
2. You never have to wonder anymore about the "what if." You now know from your own actions, and you have the results to make informed decision. You know how to either tweak the plan if you are going to do it again or what to avoid in

your plan for your next attempt. No more guessing what will happen, which is a win for your future decisions.

3. You can change your mind and change your method. Failure and setbacks are not final. This could be an opportunity to choose the road of change and experience new chances at success.

If it does not work, that does not automatically mean starting from scratch or square one again. It may mean changing one or two elements of your existing strategy. Stick to what works and what is still aligned with your vision and purpose, but be open to allowing changes for your changes.

As you make changes to your strategies, you might be okay with letting go of what does not work for you regardless of whether it is what works for everyone else. The goal here is incorporating changes that will assist you in reaching your definition of success while staying in line with your vision and purpose.

What About Money?

No matter the topic, most conversations tend to come back to how something impacts the dollars and cents. Working in accounting and tax for more than twenty years and witnessing money from various viewpoints, I can honestly say that money is whatever you want to make it mean to you within your life.

Will change help your money? Will change harm your wealth? This is where I found the advice from the Apostle Paul to be the most profound. Regardless of when change happens to us and if that change will result in having less or plenty, we are advised to find contentment during our transformations. Whatever financial state we find ourselves in during our shifting seasons, we must acknowledge that our money at the time was necessary for our greater good and our outcomes at the end of the road of change.

Defining financial success for yourself will help you further embrace the ups and downs of your money experiences within your business and your life. For one person, financial success might be the ability to be home every night by six p.m. for family dinners, living debt-free. But for another person, nothing will feel like financial success until that person is a billionaire. For someone else, financial success means having all bills on auto pay without worrying or looking if the account has enough money to send the payments. For another person, financial success means multiple six figures or a million-dollar net worth. The answer will be different for every person.

What is your contentment money number? Do you have one? And if you never reached that number, are you doing something right now in your life that still makes you feel wealthy and of value?

Money comes and goes. Sometimes, the plans will have money pouring in. Other times, even when all your efforts are meticulously calculated for each quarter, the money will either trickle in or come to a complete stop for a season. But that should not deter you from evolving and doing something worthwhile that transcends money.

Be compensated for what you do, the services you provide, and the products you sell as you deserve to live—and live well. But make sure you are being fully paid in every way and that those gains you receive as you orchestrate the changes in your life and business include inner prosperity along with currency deposits. Higher callings typically will provide you with essential abundance.

Preserve Your Positive Perspective

So far on my journey down this road of change, it has been a masterclass of how I respond to obstacles, shifts, and turns. Change does not happen without moments of challenges. More importantly, change reveals many of one's doubts, insecurities, and fears.

But it is in these moments that I do two things, and I encourage you to do them as well. One, I remember how much I have already endured, overcame, and achieved thus far—and I am still here. The same goes for you. We forget to give ourselves credit for being brave enough to even want to change. It requires faith in yourself to take those initial steps to start changing. That takes courage, and you have it, just like you had courage in the past when you completed other changes in your life. You will progress to the other side of this change as well.

Two, I choose to be thankful that I can choose to change. As a woman who is a wife, even in modern times, there are still places in this world where it would be against the law for me to make choices for myself. As a black woman who is four generations removed from slavery and whose mother was a child raised during the end of Jim Crow, I do not take for granted that I now live in a time where I can create as little or as much as I want for my life. Although there is still much work to do economically, socially, and legally to foster most equality among people, the silver lining is every day the growing possibilities of creating the life of your dreams are only limited by your imagination and creativity.

Preserve your joy. Notice I did not say happiness because happiness usually relies on what happens to you whereas joy is your own inner peace and contentment about yourself and your life. Joy is gratitude in your attitude. Joy cannot be taken from you or altered as you travel down the road of change because it is your own outlook on how things are shaping up with your life and the directions you are taking. When others cannot see the vision and the purpose you are walking toward, continue to bask in your joy knowing that once others see it for themselves you will have already changed.

Seek Support

Whenever I am making significant shifts in either my life or my business, I do not work in a complete silo. I seek support. However, I believe in various kinds of support. There is inner support, technical support, practical support, and journey support.

Inner support is usually my time to listen to my inner voice. It is my time to trust my intuition and to allow my vision and goals to not be sullied by outside perspectives and opinions. I will journal everything I am thinking during this time.

My inner support is also when I pray over what I wrote. My faith is my fortress, and it has covered me every step along the way in times of change and standing still. I know Who carries me through all things.

I then research who or what can support what I do not know, and I then begin to craft my technical support. Depending on the change I am experiencing at the moment determines the makeup of the technical support I will use. But this support usually consists of books, do-it-yourself courses, templates, and sometimes coaches or consultants.

Next, because I love my family and my home life, plus I have commitments outside of my business, I coordinate my practical support—do I need babysitters, and at what time? How will I still make it to my other scheduled events if I am about to take on this new project? Can I delegate another task to my husband or other family members or a friend to help? What can I automate or do virtually? Do I just need a nap? I believe that community helps in everyday life tasks. Just how I lean on my community for support, I offer support as well as reciprocity, which is important.

Lastly, I reassess the support I fostered as I travel down the road of change to determine if I require any other help to either accelerate the changes I am experiencing or better manage the support I require as I change. If so, that's when I might seek another book, podcast, conference, mentor, or coach to get me to where I want to go.

Support looks different for everyone. I shared how I personally break down support for myself. I cannot stress enough that I am not ever using all these resources all at once at any time. But I am aware that in one scenario, an app might be the support I need. In another scenario, I might need a coach. In another scenario, a nap does a multitude of wonderful things.

When you are going through changes, the biggest takeaway here is to know that you are not alone in your journey. Typically, many insights and lessons from experienced, like-minded people can help you avoid common mistakes or accelerate your steps. But knowing you can find help in other resources, technology, and people makes going through change not such a daunting task.

So, do I feel like I am near the end of my own journey down the road of change as I am making significant shifts in my business and life? I will leave you with this: I know the moment that I reach the end of this current journey down the road of change, I will be faced with a new crossroads to test my higher vision and purpose.

Even I am curious of when will be the day I stay on the path of what I've always done. But the road of change is filled with such enticement of many delightful surprises of self-discovery that I remain curious as to what the new incarnation of vision and purpose will be—whether it leads to less or plenty. And I am okay with that.

Meet the Author | Shan-Nel D Simmons, EA MBA

Shan-Nel D. Simmons, EA MBA, is a seasoned professional with an impressive background in accounting and finance. With more than twenty years of experience in the field, Shan-Nel has built a successful career as a tax expert and financial consultant. Her expertise and knowledge have saved hundreds of thousands of dollars for clients across the United States, Puerto Rico, and the U.S. Virgin Islands.

Before delving into the world of entrepreneurship, Shan-Nel worked as a corporate accountant, gaining invaluable insight into the financial workings of large organizations. She then transitioned into a role as an Internal Revenue Service (IRS) revenue agent, where she conducted tax audits, honing her skills in navigating complex tax laws and regulations. This experience gave her a unique perspective on the challenges faced by taxpayers and inspired her to establish her own venture, Nel Tax and Financial Solutions, where she currently serves as the founder and chief executive officer. As a federally licensed enrolled agent, Shan-Nel is recognized for her expertise in taxation and represents clients before the IRS.

With a passion for education, Shan-Nel holds multiple degrees in accounting and finance. She possesses an exceptional understanding of the intricacies of the financial industry and has honed her skills in tax problem-solving. Her dedication to staying current with industry trends and regulations enables her to provide the highest level of service to her clients.

Furthermore, Shan-Nel has a passion for sharing her expertise and knowledge with others. As a former trainer for other agents at the IRS, she has helped develop and enhance the skills of numerous professionals and business owners as it relates to taxes. She has also facilitated in-person and virtual personal finance and economic development workshops that equip individuals and businesses to make informed financial decisions and actions.

Shan-Nel has also been sought after as a keynote speaker, panelist, and trainer. Her dynamic speaking style and ability to translate complex financial concepts into easily understandable terms have made her a desirable presenter for events.

In addition to her successful career in finance, Shan-Nel is also an accomplished author. As an Amazon bestselling co-author of *Speak Up; The Ultimate Guide to Dominate in the Speaking Industry* and other books, she shares her insights and knowledge with aspiring industry professionals. Her book *A.S.K.ing for Success: My Faith Walk from Employee to Entrepreneur,* showcases Shan-Nel's personal journey and offers valuable lessons of her journey from being an employee to establishing her own successful business for those seeking to achieve success in their own entrepreneurial endeavors.

Shan-Nel's hard work and dedication have been recognized by numerous prominent publications and organizations. As an award-winning entrepreneur, she has been featured in Credit Karma, Lendio, *SHEEN* magazine, Black Speakers Network, BestCompany.com, Maryland Public Television, and *HuffPost*, among others. Her accomplishments and contributions to her field have not gone unnoticed.

Outside of her professional achievements, Shan-Nel cherishes her roles as a wife and mother. She is also a proud member of Zeta Phi Beta Sorority, Incorporated, and remains actively involved in community service. In her free time, Shan-Nel enjoys spending quality time with friends, immersing herself in smooth jazz music, and sharing hearty laughs. She lives near her hometown, Baltimore, Maryland.

CONTACT INFO:

www.neltaxandfinancialsolutions.com
www.shanneldsimmons.com
info@ntfsglobal.com
www.instagram.com/ntfsglobal
www.youtube.com/@ntfsglobal
www.linkedin.com/in/shanneldsimmons/

Crossroad Chronicles
Inner Wisdom for Life's Uncharted Territories
Crystal R. Jones, LCSW

I n the vibrant tapestry of our life's journey, it often feels like we are standing at a crossroads. It is a place that can make us question our capabilities, our dreams, and the very essence of our being. It is the place where we as women often find ourselves, wondering if we're truly ready for the journey ahead—do we have what it takes? It is a place where the Spirit whispers and sometimes shouts, urging us to take a leap of faith.

I have been there repeatedly, right at that intersection, feeling the fear that comes with making significant life and career decisions. For me, it can initially feel like my little inner child throwing a complete temper tantrum and sounding the alarm, asking, *Why? I like it here. I don't want to go!* We have all encountered those moments where our inner fear, doubt, and hesitation arise, threatening to hold us back due to intense fear of rejection, judgment, or embarrassment.

It was not too long ago that I remember writing down my heartfelt desires: I yearned to work less while making more, to embark on adventures that would take me and my family around the globe, to savor the sweet taste of freedom in how I spent my time, and to escape the ceaseless hustle of striving that had been my constant companion. These were not just thoughts tucked away; they were dreams I enthusiastically shared with my closest girlfriends and loved ones. At the time, I don't think I was aware of how to actively pursue these goals. I just knew the desires had begun to take root within my heart. Little did I know that the connections I was nurturing and the work I was passionately pursuing would soon become the keys to unlocking doors I had not even realized existed.

You see, every time a shift happens in our lives, the answers to our questions are found in our deepest desires, or as a good friend of mine says, "What did you pray for?" But be prepared for those answers to manifest in ways you might not expect. Sometimes it is a cleansing, a letting go of things you thought you wanted to hold on to. Other times, it is the realization that what you asked for comes with a price —more responsibility, better time management, and a call for additional resources to support the vision. In these moments of change, we discover that the path to our deepest desires can be a mix of letting go and taking on new responsibilities—a real-life dance of self-discovery.

Let me take you back years ago when I decided to take the plunge into the world of entrepreneurship for the very first time. Oh, the excitement was palpable, and support was pouring in from all directions because people knew me and they trusted my work. The possibilities for growth seemed endless, until they didn't. What had started as exciting plans on paper began to balloon at a rate that our small team simply could not keep up with. Eventually, it led to us falling short on our promises. The disappointment was like a heavy weight on my shoulders that reprimanded me saying, "They trusted you, and you let them down." It felt like a setback, and I could not help but carry that burden. But even in the midst of that dark period, I stumbled upon something I did not expect—a face-off with my greatest fear, the fear of failing spectacularly in front of everyone. Little did I know this challenge would become the stage where I faced and conquered some of my deepest fears head-on. It was like looking in the mirror and seeing myself staring right back, and let me tell you, it was a journey ahead that I never saw coming.

Looking back, that venture and its unexpected outcome served as a pivotal moment in my story. You see, failure stings—at times, it feels like something too immense to recover from. It is as if you want to run, hide, and never show your face again. Further, I don't remember anyone sharing what we now hear all the time, how failure is a part of the journey. All I know is that when the endeavor I had invested my heart, soul, expectations, and joy into did not unfold as expected, it felt like the ground beneath me was crumbling internally. Disappointment and self-doubt took the reins, and I questioned if I had made a colossal mistake by putting myself out there. I now know that is just how those wise inner parts of us operate. When they are overrun by embarrassment and disappointment from life's curveballs, they get into protective mode saying, "We won't try that ever again!" It's their way of trying to protect us from the perceived threat of getting hurt or failing or the potential pain of public scrutiny and disappointment.

Little did I know this experience would become the catalyst for how I viewed and experienced failure. Instead of endorsing those cries from the parts of me that demanded "never again," I began to learn more about their protective nature and the inner wisdom they held for me as I moved forward. At the heart of their concerns, those parts of me very lovingly wanted to know that I could handle the backlash even though it hurt. I reassured them that not only could I handle it, but I lovingly let those parts of me know that we could do it together. With this newfound understanding, I embarked on uncharted territory, where there was more for me to learn and experience, all while learning to navigate this course together with my "inner allies."

I emerged from that experience with a taste of what it was like to plan, create, and give birth to something, experiencing some success in the process. Despite its imperfections and the outcome diverging from my initial expectations, I did it. And you know what? Though it was short-lived, I found myself drawn to that taste of success enough to hold on to it as a possibility for the future. The seed had been planted, and when the opportunity arose once more, I made a vow to approach it differently, determined to bring a fresh perspective.

Now, don't get me wrong: This may sound like I jumped right up and was automatically empowered to do it all again. But the truth is, it took about a year of tending to those parts that felt defeated and scared, cultivating some courage along the way. Finally, with the message that those parts of me had recovered and with lots of encouragement from friends and loved ones, I ventured into the world of private practice for mental health therapy. I opened a part-time solo private practice, seeing three to four clients after my full-time job. As I reflect on it, I did not fully grasp what it could become or where it might lead. It was a dream come true to see people interested and scheduling appointments for my services. Before I knew it, my schedule was full, and I was thriving as a private practice owner. There was just one problem: I still had my full-time job.

That job provided a stable income, benefits, and paid leave. Summers off were a cherished and welcomed respite that I did not think I could live without or get elsewhere. All these comforts felt consistent and most importantly (or so I thought) safe, like the threads of a comfy security blanket that I was convinced I could not live without. However, as I tuned into the whispers of the universe, those gentle nudges urging me to move, to trust, and to explore the uncharted territory beyond that crossroads grew louder. They challenged the very notion of what "safety" meant for me in my life and began to tug at those threads of my security blanket in a way that I could not ignore.

Now, listen, I don't hear Spirit audibly, but I feel its guiding hand when it is time to make a move. It is as if I have learned all I can in my current space, and I am no longer feeling challenged. Sometimes I notice feeling limited in how I can use my gifts. Other times, it may be sheer boredom with things that I used to experience excitement and wonder around. It is like a persistent voice or knowing, gently nudging me to pay attention. This voice is also accompanied by this unmistakable shift in the atmosphere that refuses to let me continue with business as usual.

When it is time for me to shift, I also notice unexpected growth opportunities that come knocking on my door, opportunities that require me to clear space for them and step out of my comfort zone. It never fails to happen in this way. And while what awaits always meets me with wonder, curiosity, and yes nervousness, I'm grateful for the awareness of God closing doors and opening new ones, making it increasingly clear that I'm building more trust and ability to walk through them, hand in hand with those once-frightened parts of myself, showing them that it's okay to move forward, to embrace the unknown.

So, with that newfound courage, I made a daring move: I left a job that I once thought would be my lifelong career and founded Life Source Counseling Center, a private practice dedicated to supporting black, indigenous, and other women of color in feeling seen, heard, and empowered on their mental health journey. Over these years, as the practice thrived and expanded, it not only provided for my family, but also became a pillar of support for others. As a mental health therapist, I have collaboratively and compassionately worked with so many women who have made life-changing transformations as a result of our work together. I have also taken on the role of mentor and supervisor to aspiring social workers in my community, built a dedicated team to manage the administrative aspects of my business, and welcomed two exceptional therapists to my practice. Now, over a decade later, I can clearly discern why taking that courageous leap of faith was not just a personal endeavor, but a shared vision. It has become evident that the ripples of my actions extend far beyond myself. Many individuals, both known and unknown, have become intricately connected to my journey of courageously stepping through those doors.

Remember those summers off that I thought I could not live without? Well, as owner of my own private practice, I have gained the power to control my schedule, allowing me to prioritize my self-care and take well-deserved vacations whenever I choose. Now believe me when I say that entrepreneurship undoubtedly comes with significant responsibilities. There are days when the tasks seem endless and the procrastinator in me wants to drop everything and backpack around the world. However, this decision has turned out to be the most rewarding gift I could have ever bestowed upon myself, setting an example for others on the importance of self-care, work boundaries, and autonomy. This newfound sense of control over my time and priorities not only benefits my well-being but also extends to those around me. I am living that for which I prayed.

But wait, there is more to this story! Taking this step opened the door for me to further invest in my learning, setting the stage for a series of remarkable and "scared out of my mind" crossroad opportunities. A few years in, I ventured into the world of Internal Family Systems (IFS) therapy—a journey that would reshape not only my personal therapy but also my work with clients. This modality became a true game changer in how I approached my relationships, my work, and ultimately how I view the world.

As you have been with me on this journey, have you been wondering about these parts, inner aspects, inner allies, and inner wisdom I have been referring to? Well, they are the heart and soul of what makes IFS therapy truly life changing. Think of it as sitting down with those parts of yourself that may feel confident and strong, or others that may carry the weight of fear, doubt, or past wounds and having a compassionate conversation. IFS therapy helps you understand those parts, hear their stories, heal, and ultimately help them to restore balance. I was introduced to IFS by a friend, and it hit me that I had been intuitively doing some version of this all along—just relating to myself in a way that has always felt guided by God and my ancestors. It turned out that there is also an entire approach dedicated to embracing these parts of ourselves and really tapping into their transformative power.

My personal experience with IFS therapy has been like peeling back the layers of an onion, slowly getting to the core of who I am and why I react to certain situations the way I do. This way of doing therapy helped me connect with the inner aspects of my personality, or parts, especially the ones that carried fear—fear of making mistakes, fear of being seen, or feeling like an impostor.

These are feelings that many of us can relate to. It is those moments when we question whether we deserve the opportunities that come our way or if we're truly good enough to be considered. Through IFS therapy, I learned to nurture these vulnerable parts of myself, like comforting a dear friend. I began to see that these parts were not my enemies but rather fragments of my past experiences and societal pressures. Investing time and focusing on myself in this way has allowed me to heal, grow, and find a deeper level of self-compassion in so many ways.

As Black women, we oftentimes carry the weight of generational expectations, societal stereotypes, and the pressure to be "strong" all the time. This approach to therapy and relating to myself has offered me and my clients a safe space to acknowledge these burdens, to understand the fears we hold, and to embrace our authentic selves holistically as women that experience a range of feelings aside from "strength" to include not good enough, tired, imposter syndrome, insecure, scared... you name it.

This way of attunement has been my guiding light, helping me navigate the crossroads with a newfound sense of self-awareness, confidence, and resilience. It has empowered me to embark on these new journeys, even when they seem daunting, because I now have the tools to not only face my fears but lovingly be with the parts of me that are holding the fear. This work has really helped me to move from "keep it moving," or bypass the ways in which my body is naturally communicating with me to pay attention, listen, or simply slow down and for that I am eternally grateful.

Equipped with these newfound tools, I began to feel a sense of comfort within myself. My inner parts were becoming more at ease, like old friends reuniting and finding common ground. I was no longer held hostage by the fears that had once paralyzed me. Instead, I felt a newfound strength to take on new challenges, the fear was still there, but it did not have that grip on me like it did previously, and that felt good.

One year, I made a promise to myself—to challenge these lingering fears and do it scared, as I often heard echoed by motivational speakers and coaches. Let's be clear. As you have read, there are no parts of me that ever willingly want to do anything I'm scared of. Nonetheless, equipped with my IFS therapist on speed dial and channeling my inner Shonda Rhimes, I embarked on a journey of saying yes to every public speaking and IFS opportunity that came my way, no matter how terrifying it seemed. I said yes to supporting trainings, yes to doing my first IFS training for a women's retreat, yes to podcast interviews, yes to doing mental health webinars with my church, yes to leading several mental health webinars for a Fortune 500 corporation. So many yeses. With each yes, I felt a growing sense of confidence in my ability to step out of the background and really step into my gifts in a more public way. More and more, I began testing the waters of public speaking and teaching. It was not always easy—being an introvert, a bit awkward, and often becoming tongue tied or having a loss of words when speaking in front of others would have me questioning if this was the right move. But my own therapy work really helped me to know that I did not need to show up perfect, I needed to show up exactly how I am and that had value, so I persisted.

And then, it happened—an unexpected invitation arrived, urging me to consider the Internal Family Systems Institute trainers' track. I was caught off guard, to say the least. The mere thought of becoming a trainer for the institute had not even registered as a possibility in my mind, even though I had been deeply entrenched in learning this model for years at this point. My internal dialogue swiftly shifted from yes to "Wait a minute. Huh?" I was comfortable in my current role of many years and felt very skilled as a psychotherapist. A new wave of familiar fears hit me hard like a wave crashing on the shore. What if I messed this up? It was another one of those crossroad moments, where the fear of the unknown once again loomed large.

Here was that same message of God saying, *You have gotten comfortable, and it is time to stretch some more.* I had excelled in my current space, but that space was never meant to be my final destination. There was another professional experience waiting for me, and this time it happened to be this new opportunity to train for the Internal Family Systems Institute.

You might find yourself wondering if these words were a divine message to me and why did God lead you to the Institute? To that I will say those answers are still unfolding. In all honesty I don't quite know why God puts us on certain paths, but I choose to believe and deeply feel there is purpose in it. Any promotion I have ever had was never just about me and my growth alone. It has always been about the collective, like an expansive web, where each connection contributes to the strength of the whole.

What I have also come to realize is that clarity brings its own guidance. When I am in alignment with the message, I never have or need to chase opportunities; they tend to find me because I am ready for them whether I feel capable or not. That is not a brag. I am always in awe of this unfolding and have grown to expect it with so much gratitude. And still, I am still learning that perfection and knowing all there is to know are not prerequisites and are hardly ever obtainable— as Mother Oprah Winfrey wisely says, "It's where preparation meets opportunity," and it seems I was unknowingly preparing all along.

My preparation involved being in learning communities, gleaming from the wisdom of my mentors and teachers, and most importantly, connecting with and understanding all the amazing parts of myself. Each time those fearful parts began to ease their grip, I found the courage to take another step forward. This is also true for you! Opportunities often come when you least expect them. It is not about being perfect, but about being prepared, consistent, taking those courageous steps forward, and a good therapist never hurts.

The glimpses of the next steps fill me with a mix of excitement and, yes, a touch of fear. I have come to realize that a healthy dose of fear and nervousness is just part of this journey. It is a reminder that I'm pushing boundaries and exploring uncharted territory, embracing change and growth—it's truly about evolution. This path empowers us to tap into our full potential, even when faced with the uncertainty of the unknown. Equally important, it is a journey of nurturing and connecting with those inner parts that harbor concerns about what lies ahead, ensuring that they join us as cherished companions on this transformative voyage.

So, to my dear beloveds who have journeyed with me and to those who have faced similar crossroads, I want you to know this: The intersection you find yourself at today is not the end of your road; it's a doorway to fresh possibilities, opportunities, and blessings far beyond what you can think or imagine. As we continue this exciting, sometimes nerve-wracking journey together, remember, whether you need to pause and connect, pull over to the side and rest, have a good cry, or bravely continue on, I am right here in your corner cheering for you every step of the way.

Meet the Author | Crystal R. Jones, LCSW

Crystal Jones is the visionary behind Life Source Counseling Center, Inc., situated in Spotsylvania, Virginia, boasting over two decades of clinical expertise as a licensed clinical social worker. In her role as the founder and chief executive officer, Crystal ardently served as a psychotherapist, specializing in creating safe spaces for women of color to address the impact of internalized generational and systemic racism. Her dedication extends to shaping the future of social work, offering clinical supervision to aspiring clinicians seeking licensure in Virginia, and providing mentorship to practitioners in private practice.

Forging a new path, Crystal has expanded her influence within her professional community, emerging as a trailblazer in the Internal Family Systems Institute (IFS-I) organization. As a highly sought-after Internal Family Systems (IFS) lead trainer and consultant, Crystal has left her mark both in the United States and abroad, conducting sessions in diverse locations such as Canada, Bali, the United Kingdom, Poland, and the West Indies. Her approach seamlessly blends a heart-led leadership with unparalleled expertise, defining her multifaceted roles within the mental health community.

Crystal R. Jones, LCSW

Crystal's expertise has garnered invitations to speak at organizations, including Boston Scientific, California Institute of Integral Studies, Delta Sigma Theta Sorority, Incorporated (Fredericksburg Alumnae Chapter), Spotsylvania County Public Schools, DC Public Schools, Institute of Contemporary Psychotherapy and Psychoanalysis, University of Wisconsin - Madison, and more. Her insights have been featured on prominent podcasts, such as *When We Speak, IFS Talks, Grief Is My Side Hustle,* and *The Truth, Love, & Beauty Podcast.*

Beyond her professional accomplishments, Crystal cherishes her role as a mother of three and a devoted wife of more than twenty years. During her downtime, she embraces life with her family and friends, enjoys international travel adventures, savoring delectable cuisines, communing with nature, and indulging in contagious laughter.

Crystal's journey exemplifies the transformative power of faith and purpose. In both professional spheres and cherished family moments, she remains a beacon of authenticity and resilience, inspiring others to embrace their unique paths.

Pivoting Mental Health Group Practices Ownership

Jennifer Cobb, LCSW, DBTC

"There is no glory in a grind that literally grinds you down to dust."

— Dr. Eve Ewing

I invite you to take a deep breath with me and now picture your loved one who struggles with their mental health. It may be your mother, your brother, your childhood best friend, your child... It may be you. They may struggle with getting out of bed, have anxiety so bad they lose job after job, or suffer greatly with chronic thoughts of suicide. Now hold them gently in your mind as we transition to thinking about their mental health clinician.

Their clinician sees six to eight clients a day—thirty to forty clients a week—in order to make "productivity goals" at the company they work for. They start out eager and full of passion. They love their work, and they care deeply for your loved one. Fast forward two or three short years. They still care deeply, but this work is hard and is taking a toll. They find themselves dreaming of throwing it all away to raise chickens and keep company with bees.

More accurately, though, it's not likely the work that is taking its toll. After all, this clinician is likely deeply passionate about this work and feels called to it strongly. More often, it is the systems that this therapist is functioning in—namely, the company that writes their paycheck. You see, many of these companies prioritize productivity goals, high caseloads, and become what some call "associate factories" because of the way that new-to-the-field associate level clinicians get hired, worked to within an inch of their wellness, and they then cycle out the door to look for something more sustainable, making these companies a revolving door of therapists, but also breeding grounds for unhealthy habits. Take this "norm" within our profession and add to it that many go into business and open practices without any formal training in leadership or business management, and you've got a recipe for recreating the same wellness-destroying practices, policies, and procedures being duplicated over and over. So, while your loved one's therapist is likely talking to them about ways to structure their life in a way that promotes healing and healthy habits, their therapist finds themselves in an environment where they're unable to do the same.

It's time that we pivot the way our mental health professionals think about and run their practices. It's time that we center wellness for our employees in the mental health sector. In order to do that, we have to provide awareness, education, and support for doing things differently. The good news is I've paved one path—this isn't something that needs to be done alone. You don't have to be the lone explorer out there, machete in hand, busting your way through overgrown wilderness. One path forward has already been cleared. Although this will likely still be a path filled with challenges, the result will be so very worth it.

In the next several pages, I'm speaking directly to individuals who are mental health providers, entrepreneurs, folks who are considering or have recently opened up a private practice and are contemplating bringing other clinicians into the creation of a group private practice.

However, folks in other positions and seasons in life may also find some gems of information that help them see something from another perspective or are in some other way useful. I'm inviting you along this hero's journey through the path of creating an employee-centered mental health practice in order to illustrate one path that may be a helpful template for creating something different and pivoting our mental health system.

While the word *hero* has a lot of implications, I'm using it here to try to capture the depth of responsibility and determination that comes with entrepreneurship, and ultimately to becoming a vehicle for carving out a way to create jobs and fill a need in your community. The journey of a leader, entrepreneur, and group private practice owner is akin to the archetypal hero's journey. Just as heroes embark on quests to bring about positive change, leaders in mental health must navigate their own unique challenges to create a transformative impact, and just like every journey, there are ups and downs, successes and failures, challenges and strength. At the core of this journey lies the concepts of value-centered and employee-centered leadership, a beacon that can guide mental health practitioners in their noble quest to heal, empower, and inspire in a way that keeps not only clients well, but employees too.

In fact, I have seen over and over again that an employee-centered model of practice increases the satisfaction and performance of employees, which in turn increases client success outcomes. In other words, by focusing on employee wellness, we have a win-win-win scenario where the practice wins by attracting and keeping high-quality, extremely skilled, valuable employees who remain committed long term; the employees win by being in an environment that they co-create, have ownership over, and feel seen and valued in.

The clients win because they step into a nurturing environment and are working with providers who are nourished and refreshed, therefore having more resources to pour into their work together.

Act One: The Call to Leadership

The hero's journey typically begins with a call to adventure, an irresistible summons to leave the comfort zone and step into the unknown. In mental health entrepreneurship, this call is often sparked by a deep sense of empathy and a desire to alleviate the suffering of others. It's the realization that the path of leadership can be a powerful means to bring about positive change in the lives of those struggling with their mental health. This call became louder and louder for me when I was working in community mental health. I actually had the unique pleasure of working with a really healthy, value-aligned non-profit organization, which is not something that many people can boast. I learned how important community is in this position and that all interactions—big and small—matter. I learned how to communicate with community partners and form informal partnerships where we could support the work we were all doing to benefit the community's wellness.

However, even within this organization that I look back on fondly today, there were still some unhealthy habits being formed. For example, there was a strong "make it happen, any way you can" mentality, which often meant putting in fifty- to sixty-hour work weeks. It was challenging to take time off because there was no one else to cover, and you often ended up working twice as hard before and after days off, that it wasn't really worth the hassle. But it was within this context that my passion became louder and louder—I saw firsthand the stigma that came from folks struggling with their mental health, and specifically those with extreme emotion dysregulation.

I heard story after story from community members about their experiences within our larger community mental health system that were often sad and infuriating, sometimes unbelievable, and once in a while, bordering on professionally unethical. I also watched closely during this time to the experiences my community colleagues were having—how long they were staying in their jobs, what their life outside of work looked like, and how valued they felt in their work. It was during this experience, mostly from watching those in other agencies, that I began to form my fire for creating something different. My goal became to open a group private practice and to build an experience that centered on the employee feeling valued. My hypothesis: employees that feel seen, heard, safe, and valued become dedicated, long-term employees who are able to build their work around their life and therefore be a healthy provider for those they work with. In other words, these healthy employees actually get better outcomes in treatment with their clients. So, centering my practice on employee wellness vicariously centers the practice on client wellness as well.

I invite you now to reflect on your own journey in this area. Have you had work experiences that actually rewarded you for unhealthy behaviors (staying late, working beyond your capacity, monetary rewards for meeting production levels that are outrageous, et cetera) and punished you for healthy behaviors (setting healthy limits, assertive communication, prioritizing family, et cetera)?

If so, my call to action for you is to consider what it would be like to create a practice that is centered on your employees. How will this be captured in your mission and vision statements? What are the top values that will guide your business decisions? What kind of employees do you want to attract, and what do they value? What does a healthy environment look like? What will you do as a leader to reward healthy actions rather than unhealthy actions? What kind of culture will you create and how?

Act Two: Crossing the Threshold

The hero in his journey crosses a threshold into a new world filled with challenges and uncertainties. Similarly, the mental health entrepreneur opening a private practice is usually taking a leap into an entirely different world. We are often not trained in business management, marketing, or networking. Most folks I see making this journey (myself included) start by thinking they are just going to go into practice to do what they love—provide therapy for clients. The plan is that the clients who need to find them will (somehow). With all of those great-fit clients that show up, the clinician will simply enjoy their time "in the chair" doing what they are passionate about and really skilled in. Then...reality. You're suddenly looking at commercial leases and attempting to decipher the legal lingo, you're developing paperwork, and trying to figure out the language that you want as well as the language that must be included to protect your business from liability. You're suddenly looking at codes and laws and figuring out how to stay current in this changing landscape, and you're noticing that this "money conversation" with your clients is a whole new experience. It starts to sink in that being a skilled clinician doesn't exactly translate into being a skilled business owner and entrepreneur. *Ooooof,* the learning curve.

My biggest takeaway during this season of my journey was that I needed to begin thinking like a business owner and shift my perspective from clinician to business owner–clinician, but that business owner had to take priority. This didn't necessarily change my actions "from the chair," but it certainly changed my actions in regard to having conversations ahead of time about insurance, fees, cancellations, et cetera. It also helped me view my practice from above, looking down on a wider view of how the systems and practices were fitting into a bigger picture. I was able to go back in and modify some language around my policies, tighten up language in my intake paperwork, and overall put things in place that helped my business run smoother, therefore my clinical work could take priority during my time with clients. I had some hard lessons learned —for example, the large, unpaid bill that grew and grew and grew because I expected that parents would "do the right thing" since I was helping them with the most precious thing in their world—their daughter. It never got paid and was a huge financial burden and lesson learned.

I learned that stretching outside of my own time boundaries rarely benefited anyone when I agreed to meet the morning of a holiday for a client in crisis who then just didn't show up. I learned that there are seasonal ebbs and flows in the practice world and how to expect, predict, and plan for them. Slowly I began developing my "entrepreneur legs" and seeing my work through that lens. However, what did not change during this transition was the deep compassion and respect that I had toward my clients. These individuals were fighting for their lives, many times swimming upstream in a mental health system that doesn't work well and often punished them for trying to get their needs met. It was becoming clearer and clearer that there is such a need to create something different—an organization that is serving those individuals who are enduring immense suffering, and to do so in a way that keeps those serving these individuals (our clinicians) well and able to sustain this work for a long time.

My call to action for you in this stage of the journey is to build your policies and procedures around the values of your practice. In other words, begin to think about how your mission, vision, and values are being "lived" in the ways that you practice, in the systems that you have in place, and the actions that you take as a business owner and entrepreneur. In addition, connect yourself to those who have created a type of practice that you admire. Find out where the information flows—where do you find out about changes in policy within insurance companies, state regulations, decisions that impact your business. I imagine that you've historically filled up your prior continuing education hours on clinical topics—consider shifting to really becoming a learner around topics such as accounting, business management, policy, marketing, and other areas that will fill the gaps. Look into entrepreneurial support options such as coaching, consulting, and other ways to begin to shift your support system to be made up of other business owners who are faced with similar challenges and decisions that you will now be facing.

Act Three: Trials and Tribulations

Throughout the hero's journey, the hero faces numerous trials and tribulations. In the realm of mental health leadership, these trials may take the form of limited resources, bureaucratic obstacles, or ethical dilemmas. True leaders remain steadfast in their commitment to their values, even when the path ahead seems arduous. Similarly, mental health entrepreneurs must navigate the complex landscape of business ownership, human resources, pay systems, client-facing systems, management systems, marketing, networking, in addition to their client services. They must possess the skills to learn about these tasks and steadily venture head-on into uncharted territories as they build the practice they are proud to run. My experience with this journey is that going in, you "don't know what you don't know," but that you quickly find out some of your blind spots. Specifically, you've now created a thriving practice and are ready to bring on other employees.

With this decision comes immense responsibility — you are now responsible for not only your client's experience, but that of your employees. The work that you've done in the previous part of your journey — identifying core values, creating systems — now gets deepened further by you creating the employee-centered model that will create the culture of wellness that you're striving to create, a pivot from most other agencies and practices and the current industry "norm."

The most important takeaway for me during this phase of entrepreneurship was the slow creation of what I now call our collaborative community model. This model takes our culture of shared commitment and ownership and boils it down into actionable steps. It's founded on all who are a part of our practice—from administrative personnel to interns to long-term clinicians to the owner—having a meaningful impact and contribution to the functioning of the entire practice. There is an expectation of contribution to the functioning of our well-oiled practice. In return, there is enormous benefit in ways that are both tangible and intangible. For example, we have an environment free from micromanaging—you are responsible for your tasks and you're trusted to do them in a way and a time that works for you.

Our systems have built-in natural consequences, so if something isn't working, there are natural consequences rather than more punitive punishments and action plans. We have a culture of setting our own pace—you decide what days, times, pace you want to work, and you build your caseload at the pace and to the amount that you want to have. No one is telling you what the right number of clients is for you to see, and no one is setting minimum caseloads. In addition, we do not engage in carceral, policing practices of folks' time and money— you take days off when you want and/or need, you manage your own money. In other words, management isn't setting aside a pool of your money for you to request at a later time for paid time off. You're getting paid all of your money, and you determine the way that works for you to manage that money. In this way, employees feel deeply valued, cared for, and seen in a way that truly encourages them to build their work around their life (and wellness).

My call to action for you in this stage of the journey is to develop systems that are both client centered and employee centered. Automate as much as you can, develop systems that are efficient and simple for clients to use, as well as systems that allow your clinicians to really focus on what they do best—clinical practice. Consider developing (or seeking consultation) around a model that is in alignment with your practice's core values. Consider our collaborative community model.

How can you have practices and policies that value your employees on multiple levels? What tangible and intangible benefits are important to your employees? How can a system of ownership be created and become a part of your collective culture? Regardless of what model you choose, consider pivoting away from the standard model that is chosen by most practices simply because "it's how it's done." Strive to center your decision making on the wellness of your employees, and the outcomes for your clients and your business as a whole will follow.

Act Four: The Mentor's Wisdom

Mentors play a crucial role in the hero's journey, guiding the hero with wisdom and insights. For your journey to creating a group practice that has pivoted from the status quo, I challenge you to look outside of our field to find mentors. While it is vastly important to keep growing your clinical skills, my guess is that you're a solid clinician if you've chosen this path to group practice ownership. Where you could likely benefit from mentorship is from folks who specialize in running a business, folks who align with your value-driven style of employee leadership, folks who have heart-centered business practices. In addition, be open to seeking mentorship from your employees and from the clients you serve. This is where my biggest learning has come from (and continues to come from) during my own journey as a group practice owner and entrepreneur. I have learned lessons in being able to sit and have challenging conversations that are rooted in compassion. I have learned lessons in being willing to hear a person's story and the impact that one of our policies or procedures had on that individual. I have learned about the patience it takes to allow someone space to make their own mistakes in order to really find their own style. I have learned that knowing my own limits for risk tolerance and setting up practices and procedures that align with that level of tolerance can help my employees have a frame to understand and experiment with their own growth.

These lessons learned have greatly impacted the culture of our practice...it is known that mistakes will happen and can be repaired without damaging relationships; that differences of opinion and perspective are actually welcomed rather than punished, and that hiring and firing practices really deeply matter to the functioning of the whole.

My call to action for you in this spirit of mentorship is to strengthen your own ability to really see your employee's strengths and have conversations with them about how to most effectively and efficiently do their job centered around those strengths. Help folks problem solve areas that they're struggling with, encourage them to think outside of the box and experiment with solutions, which also takes creativity, patience, and non-judgment.

If you have a valuable and committed employee who is struggling in one area of their job but really shines in other areas, consider restructuring around their strengths. This takes active effort on your end and really knowing your employees, but the outcome will be that your employees will really know that you see them and value them. Consider ways that you can nurture relationships both individually and as a whole.

Act Five: Transformation and Self-discovery

As the hero progresses on their journey, they undergo profound transformations. Mental health leaders also experience personal growth as they learn to harness their strengths, confront their weaknesses, and develop the resilience needed to navigate the challenges of their field. In this stage of building my group private practice, I was really able to sit and look at "who's here—and who's not here." What voices are we missing, what individuals with lived experiences do we have and do we not have? In this stage, intentional hiring became very important, and it was absolutely essential that I created a hiring committee that could all provide their wisdom in the interviewing and hiring process. We got even better at honing in on identifying "areas of genius" and really encouraging growth in those different areas, as well as gifting others on the team with their wisdom. We really settled deeply into our model of circular leadership and highlighted constantly that everyone is bringing something unique and valuable and that degree, years of experience, and other ways of measuring seniority don't apply to our practice.

In this employee-centered model and experience, employees know deeply that they matter—if they leave, there will be a shift in the whole of the practice because they are there and are a part of the whole. The practice is different, forever changed because of their voice, contribution, and commitment. This works against the status quo of some other organizations where "everyone is replaceable." This really helps us solidify the reality of "we are better as a whole because you are here, with your unique gifts, lived experiences, perspectives, and voice."

This also is the stage where I became aware of the unlearning and relearning process that was necessary for employees entering our agency. Most folks come in having already learned "norms" from other places of employment, and we recognized the need to speak about the difference, invite unlearning of habits, and actively encourage folks to think about this work differently from the start.

My call to action for you in this stage is to invite your clinicians to work within their zone of genius. Continue your thinking of a practice owner—begin to settle into your role of being the visionary for your organization and delegate tasks to those who can complete them more efficiently and effectively than you can. Continue to build your dream team.

Act Six: The Return and Impact

In the final act of the hero's journey, the hero returns home transformed and ready to share their newfound wisdom and gifts with their community. Similarly, value-centered mental health leaders create employee-centered practices with a deeper understanding of their purpose and a commitment to creating positive change in the lives of their employees, clients, and the broader community. This remains the work that it takes to be doing something different within a community that already has a standard way of functioning. This takes the ongoing work of settling into your values, helping yourself and others consistently unlearn and relearn healthier ways of being in relationship with their career, and having the courage and the humility to continually assess and reflect.

My call to action to you here is to remember your loved one who you held in your mind from the beginning of our time together—this loved one who is putting their trust in another to help them with their mental health. It makes absolute sense to want their clinician to be well, valued and cared for so that they can pass on that nurturing and presence to their clients. I encourage all of you who are embarking on your own journey to group practice ownership to consider joining those of us who have pivoted the way that we build practices—and to strive from the start to center in employee wellness in a way that creates a win-win-win outcome for your employees, your clients, and your practice.

Jennifer Cobb, LCSW, DBTC

Meet the Author | Jennifer Cobb, LCSW, DBTC

Jennifer Cobb, LCSW, DBTC, is the owner of Guilford Counseling, PLLC, in Greensboro, North Carolina. Jennifer has built a thriving group private practice that specializes in comprehensive Dialectical Behavior Therapy (DBT) and trauma-informed practice and takes great pride in the unique community collaborative model that has been co-created organically. Jennifer provides training to other clinicians interested in becoming intensively trained in DBT from a trauma-focused lens and is an adjunct professor in the joint master of social work program between the University of North Carolina at Greensboro and North Carolina Agricultural & Technical State University. In addition, Jennifer has built a robust coaching and consulting practice where she specializes in helping clinicians build value-centered and employee-centered private and group practices. You can find more information at www.guilfordcounseling.com or www.collaborativegrouppractice.com.

The "You" Turn

Dana Wilson

Enough was enough. I no longer wanted to live into my foreseeable future. I desired something different—a future that was unknown, but it was calling me. You know that feeling, don't you? That tugging at your soul that tells you there's more—more to life, more to you, more to everything. It's like a whisper in the wind, so easy to ignore but impossible to forget.

It was 11:59 p.m. on December 31, 1995. I took my last drag of that good ole Newport cigarette. I decided in that moment I was going to give myself a chance—a chance at a life bigger, better, and bolder. This was no ordinary New Year's resolution. It was an existential pivot, a "you" turn, if you will. The clock struck midnight, and in the silence that followed, I heard the echoes of my past and the melodies of my future harmonizing in the most beautiful way.

The very next day, my nose could not stand the smell of smoke nor ashes. I had to clear my space of any remnants of that habit of the past. My mind, body, and spirit had shifted. Gone were the days of living in discord. See, while my body enjoyed the cigarette, my mind knew that it was unhealthy, and my spirit was disappointed with every puff.

Our mind, body, and spirit components are connected. They thrive when in harmony. It's like they're a dream team, each with a specialized role but all striving for the same championship—your ultimate well-being. Your mind is the strategist, laying out game plans and always scanning for opportunities. The body is the star athlete, physical and ready, responding with precision to the mind's signals. And your spirit? It's the heart of the team, the motivational captain who reminds everyone why they're in the game in the first place.

To this present day, the decision to quit smoking cigarettes is one of the top five pivotal choices I have made. This was probably the first time I consciously allowed myself to be an active participant in my life. I chose me by harnessing the power of aligning my mind, body, and spirit together. The exhilaration of this newfound freedom was unparalleled. There's nothing quite like taking control of your destiny, even if it begins with something as seemingly insignificant as quitting a bad habit. But let's get something straight: It's never insignificant if it changes the course of your life.

Can you think back to a time when you made a decision that was just a whisper in your mind, and you turned it into action? A time when you brought an abstract thought into tangible reality? When you not only decided to follow through but actually did it? Think about it. Let it sink in. Decisions have ripple effects that touch not only you but also the people around you. My choice to quit smoking led to clearer thinking, healthier living, and a more profound spiritual understanding. It made me realize the importance of choice and responsibility, not just for myself but for my loved ones too.

Have you identified your own potential "you" turn—your moment to pivot, to change direction for the better? Your ultimate dream team— your mind, body, and spirit—are waiting on the sidelines, ready to play their hearts out for you. They're just waiting for you to put them in the game. Are you ready to harness their potential?

Action Steps

Now, why are these action steps essential? Well, think of them as a roadmap to personal transformation. They guide you through the process of turning your "you" turn from a mere concept into a living, breathing reality. Each step is designed to move you closer to a life of harmony and fulfillment.

Identify your discord: What is that thing that's out of harmony in your life?

Set a goal: It doesn't have to be big, but it has to be meaningful.

Activate your dream team: Consistently engage your mind, body, and spirit in this endeavor.

Be an active participant: Take the wheel; you're the one steering your life.

Celebrate your pivotal choices: Acknowledge your wins, no matter how small they may seem.

The "you" turn is a phenomenon we all encounter at some point, an invitation to take a new direction in the winding road of life. For me, that turn started with the decision to extinguish a cigarette, and in doing so, ignite a new way of living that involved harmonizing my mind, body, and spirit. That turn on that fateful New Year's Eve was not just a change in direction, it was a complete shift in how I participated in my own life story.

So, what's your "you" turn going to be?

Allow me to share another pivotal "you" turn that came years later, as if to say that life constantly offers us these opportunities for profound pivots. During my years of active duty in the Air Force, I found myself at yet another crossroads. My dual roles—as someone committed to military service and as a mother to a special needs son—were pulling me in directions that seemed increasingly irreconcilable.

I was wearing thin, a candle burning at both ends. When at work, my son's well-being preoccupied my thoughts, and when I was with him, concerns about my military duties clouded my focus. My body was also waving a white flag of surrender, signaling it couldn't keep up with the relentless pace. I was so out of sync that I even ended up spraining my ankle.

During this tumultuous time, it felt as if my mind, body, and spirit were singing in unison, but not in the way you'd hope—they were unified in sheer exhaustion. I was on autopilot, functioning on fumes.

Just when I thought I was nearing the end of my rope, a lifeline was thrown my way. A probing question from a stranger disrupted my mental fog: "Have you ever thought that maybe your military service and your family's needs are no longer compatible?"

This was an idea I had never even allowed myself to consider. But as soon as the thought was voiced, it resonated with me like a gong, demanding my full attention.

This epiphany was another monumental "you" turn in my journey. The realization that I had the power to redefine my career path for the sake of a healthier work-life balance was liberating. So, it was as if a newfound energy and a sense of possibility had been breathed into me, giving me the courage to contemplate a different way of living—of being. Giving myself permission to consider another way. This was another chapter in my ongoing journey of aligning my mind, body, and spirit for the sake of a more fulfilling, balanced life.

Now, let's turn the spotlight back to you. When you look at the crossroads ahead, what kind of "you" turn calls to you? What shifts, large or small, await you in your own tapestry of life? You see, the road of life doesn't stop offering these twists and turns. They'll keep coming, nudging you toward growth and new experiences. But here's the thing: making those "you" turns is not always a walk in the park.

It is my belief that life will continue to require "you" turns if you desire to thrive and live on purpose. Don't get me wrong, these turns are anything but easy. We get comfortable in our established patterns, settling into the illusion of safety and predictability. In doing so, we sometimes forget our own strength and resilience, the very attributes that once empowered us to make bold moves.

There are moments when our life experiences, particularly the challenging ones, paralyze our memory of what we had once courageously achieved. Maybe you've been knocked down a few times, and you're hesitant to get back up. Maybe your self-doubt whispers louder than your confidence, sowing seeds of uncertainty. Maybe you're bound by past failures, or perhaps it's the societal norms and expectations that tether you.

We place mental roadblocks, inventing endless reasons not to act— "It's too much," "I'm too old," "I don't have the time," "What will people say?" "I can't afford to fail." All these internal and external voices muddle our clarity, obstructing the alignment of mind, body, and spirit.

But here's the crucial point—these challenges, as real and imposing as they may seem, are also the gates that guard something precious. They safeguard our potential, our ability to be better, do better, and live better. To push through, you've got to get your mind, body, and spirit back in sync, like the unbeatable team they're meant to be.

Your mind has to rise above the racket, to strategize, to focus on the goals, and discern the viable paths toward them. Your body needs to follow suit, energized, and ready to act on those plans. And your spirit? It needs to become the driving force, the reservoir of faith and determination, reminding you why you began this journey in the first place.

Remember, every "you" turn is an invitation, not just to change direction but to evolve, to become more fully the person you're meant to be. Yes, the alignment of mind, body, and spirit takes work, but it's work that pays off in immeasurable ways, offering a richer, more fulfilling life.

So, as you stand at your next crossroad, will you take the turn?

Take it from me, I know it's not easy, but you can do this.

When I granted myself the freedom to contemplate leaving the military—a path I knew like the back of my hand—it was no cakewalk. I was stepping away from financial stability, a structured environment, and a career path that had been laid out for me. I was stepping into the unpredictable world of entrepreneurship, but it was a calculated risk, one taken to be more present in my life, not just as a mother but as an individual seeking personal and professional growth.

The shift from military discipline to the volatile landscape of entrepreneurship felt like jumping off a cliff and assembling my parachute on the way down. Every day brought new challenges—some that questioned my capability and others that tested my resolve. But here's where that magical alignment of mind, body, and spirit came back into play.

My mind had to be sharp, continually evolving, forever learning. The strategizing never stopped. Whether it was market research, understanding consumer behavior, or simply keeping up with the latest industry trends, my mental game had to be on point. My body, too, had to adapt to this new normal. Gone were the days of a rigid military schedule. Now, the physical demands varied from intense periods of work to adaptability and quick maneuvering.

And let's not forget the spirit, that ever-present force guiding me through the highs and the lows. Whenever I doubted myself or the journey I had undertaken, it was my spirit that reminded me of my why, my core reason for taking this colossal leap in the first place.

The commitment to my dreams had to be unwavering. I had to remain compliant with the plans I'd outlined, sticking to my strategies, and continually reassessing as situations changed.

Consistency became my mantra, ensuring that every day I took steps that moved me closer to my goals.

So, in this ongoing pursuit of fulfillment, remember this: Challenges are not roadblocks; they're stepping stones. Each one is an opportunity to recalibrate, to fine-tune that alignment of mind, body, and spirit, and to fortify your resolve. The journey might be fraught with uncertainty, but the destination? Oh, it's worth every struggle, every doubt, every sacrifice.

It's the fruition of a life lived on purpose, a life where every strand counts.

Your next "you" turn is waiting. Are you ready to embrace it?

Whether it's embarking on a journey to hair growth, pursuing a Sisterlocks business like I did, or finding your purpose, the harmony of mind, body, and spirit is a principle that can be universally applied. It's not just about the big, life-altering decisions. It's also about the small, daily choices that contribute to your overall well-being. When you make you a priority, when you listen to what you need in every facet of your life, that's when you start to see transformation.

Let's start by looking at a journey to hair growth. It's not merely a physical transformation; it's deeply entangled with your mind, body, and spirit. For example, your mind needs to be educated on what's going on in your body, what works for your specific hair type, the nutrients essential for hair growth, and the products that are most beneficial. Your body takes part through consistent care routines, while your spirit feels rejuvenated with every positive change, uplifting your self-confidence. The harmony of these three components can result in not just stronger, healthier hair but a more self-assured, vibrant you.

Pursuing a Sisterlocks business is another excellent example. Your mind needs to absorb the technical skills, understand the market, and strategize for business growth. Your body participates through the physical act of creating those Sisterlocks, standing for hours as you intricately lay the foundation of your client's hair. Meanwhile, your spirit is engaged by the creative joy and sense of accomplishment, not to mention the cultural and emotional significance that many people attach to their hair. The rewards are not just financial but also emotional and psychological. You have the satisfaction of building something from the ground up, witnessing its growth, and knowing that it directly stems from your efforts.

Finding your purpose is a more intangible but equally powerful journey. When your mind, body, and spirit are aligned in your quest to discover your purpose, every setback becomes a set-up for a comeback—every challenge a new lesson. The rewards of finally knowing why you're here can bring incomparable joy and peace to your spirit. You'll find work no longer feels like "work," stress diminishes, and every day becomes more fulfilling.

Benefits of Making You a Priority

Physical Well-being: When you're in tune with your body, you can more easily spot irregularities and address them before they become severe issues.

Emotional Stability: Taking time to check in with your feelings and mental state helps to stave off stress, depression, and anxiety, making room for more joy and tranquility.

Clarity of Purpose: The alignment of mind, body, and spirit brings a clearer understanding of your goals and your path to achieving them.

Increased Productivity: A healthy mind in a healthy body is more focused and efficient, leading to improved productivity in every endeavor, whether personal or professional.

Enhanced Relationships: When you're well-balanced and happy, it positively affects your relationships. You're better equipped to communicate, empathize, and connect with others.

Rewards

Self-confidence: Achieving small and big goals when your mind, body, and spirit are aligned boosts your self-confidence. You start believing more in your capabilities.

Personal Satisfaction: There's an innate joy that comes from accomplishing something solely for yourself.

Resilience: As you overcome challenges, you build resilience, preparing yourself for whatever life throws your way next.

Gratification

The gratification of making you a priority is both immediate and long-lasting. Instantly, you feel better—happier, healthier, and more centered. In the long term, you're setting yourself up for a life that's not just livable, but enjoyable, purposeful, and meaningful.

So, whatever your "you" turn might be—be it small changes like adopting a healthier lifestyle or significant shifts like changing your career or starting a business—know that the harmony of mind, body, and spirit is your unfailing compass, guiding you toward a life where every strand truly counts.

And so, I leave you with this: Our lives are a series of turns, pivots, and "you" turns. The beauty of it lies in our ability to steer ourselves in new directions, even when the road ahead seems foggy. We've all had those 11:59 p.m. moments, like the one that led me to snuff out that last cigarette. The journey didn't end there; it merely set me on a course that opened new horizons, from personal growth to a life-altering realization during my military service.

Let's get real for a moment. Can you relate? Have you ever felt stuck, only to realize that the choice to move forward was in your hands all along? It's easy to forget that we are the authors of our own stories, complete with the power to write new chapters.

Think about this: Your mind, body, and spirit are like an all-star team, each offering a unique set of skills but collectively working toward the same goal—your well-being. When they're in sync, their potential is limitless. However, when there's discord, it feels like your life is a rudderless ship. It's that internal alignment, your dream team working in harmony, that makes all the difference.

So, here's your call to action. Are you ready to take your "you" turn? I promise you, it's more than just a change of direction; it's an invitation to live authentically, to show up fully in your life. It's the pivot that takes you from existing to truly living.

Your Action Steps Revisited

Identify the dissonance: What's pulling you away from your true self?

Set your intention: Define what a harmonious life looks like for you.

Engage your dream team: Involve your mind, body, and spirit in your transformation.

Be the active participant: Don't just make choices, act on them.

The "You" Turn

Savor your wins: Every change, no matter how small, is a step in the right direction.

In the grand scheme of things, the ability to make pivotal choices and shifts, however big or small, defines who we are and what we become. Whether it's quitting a bad habit or recalibrating your life's priorities, each "you" turn is a new beginning, a fresh page.

So, what's your next chapter going to be? Remember, you have the pen. Write a story that you'll be proud to tell. Let's make every strand count.

Meet the Author | Dana Wilson

Dana Wilson is a certified trichologist, Sisterlocks educator, certified empowerment coach, certified BIO research assistant, certified cold capper, veteran, author, and more importantly a mother of a son on the autism spectrum. Dana has a bachelor's degree in business administration. She is the director and chief executive officer of Hair Cares Inc., which provides in-person and virtual hair growth services, Sisterlocks business consulting, and personal coaching.

Dana's mission is to empower audacious women with an understanding that Every Strand Counts by piecing mind, body, and spirit components together, which result in scalp rejuvenation, hair regeneration, and a growing sustainable Sisterlocks business. She encourages wholistic living and full self-expression, through hair advocacy, training, coaching, consulting, books, and the talk show *Every Strand Counts*.

The Pivot's True Meaning

Vinara "VEE" Mosby

Over time, I came to understand that pivoting was not just about changing careers or pursuing new passions. It was about adapting to life's twists and turns, finding strength in vulnerability, and embracing the unknown. My father's passing had been a profound loss, but it had also been a catalyst for my own growth and transformation.

It was January 2019, and I had started my day. Friday was a normal working day with a few early-morning clients. Then I met an old friend for lunch. What a great time we had. We talked about old and current times, our kids, what we were doing in life. We talked about everything. Lunch was two hours of a great time. I told my friend how I could not wait to tell my dad that I saw him. You see, until his passing, my dad and his dad were great friends. He had not seen him nor his mom in some time. So, what did I do? I called my dad to tell him about who I had lunch with. He didn't answer, but that was not unusual because he was always doing something. He was a very active senior. As a matter of fact, he was supposed to have been a pallbearer at his classmate's mom's homegoing service that afternoon, so when he didn't answer, I naturally thought he would call me back. It was okay. I ran a few more errands and then I went home.

About 5:30 p.m., my brother called me and told me to go to Dad's house now. I was like, "Why? What's happening?" He didn't know. He just said something was wrong with Dad, and I needed to go down there right now. I called my dad's friend, and she was crying/moaning, I just couldn't figure it out. She put a man on the phone, and he asked me who I was and how long would it take for me to get there. My reply was twenty minutes. Meanwhile, I had a friend over, and she spoke to the gentleman on the phone for a few seconds as my son and I were getting our shoes and keys.

We left, scared and not quite sure of what to expect, but I drove as fast as I could. About seven minutes after I left home, my mom called and asked me why weren't they taking my dad to the hospital. I told her I didn't know. She knew. She was a retired medical professional. Death wasn't anything she hadn't seen before. I do believe it hit her differently this time.

We arrived. I was greeted by my brother's best friend and a fireman with a policeman waiting at the door. I wanted to go to my dad's bedroom. They were adamant.

"You don't want to see him like that. We need to finish doing what we are doing. Please wait out here."

I instantly became numb. Eventually, they told me that I could go back. All I could do was rub his hand as my daughter was rubbing his feet while everyone else was standing around watching, probably thoughts of unbelief flowing through their minds. It was certainly unbelievable to me. And to this day, I still have no regrets about seeing him lying there.

My life had changed. That is the one thing I knew for sure.

The Pivot's True Meaning

We celebrated his life as if he were here. More than three hundred people came to express their condolences and celebrate with us. Those who talked to him regularly would tell me how proud of me he was. Of course I would say, "That is so kind of you to say." I thought differently, I guess. At that very moment, who knew what he thought. I just knew this wasn't a dream anymore.

Sunday was the real first day of a brand-new world and life without my father. I had to hold things together now in case he came back. I wanted him to be proud of me because I was taking care of things. Crazy I know, but then I was internally clueless. It was all a part of the mourning process. We all mourned in our very different ways. Our choices and decisions, our actions and outcomes, our highs and lows were a direct result of the fact that we all were mourning. And we mourned silently when we should have all been mourning together. We all had lost someone very dear and special to us. Instead, we became each other's enemy. That made everything worse. What I realized is it happens more than anyone can ever imagine.

The next days and months were very interesting to say the least. I had to move on about life but could not figure out how I was going to move on. Every day, first thing in the morning, I would cry for several minutes and then I would randomly cry throughout my day. *Lord, help me* would be my prayer. *Lord, guide, direct, and please give me strength* became my daily mantras. I believe He said one step and one day at a time. I was still numb.

Over the following months, I spent many days at my father's house going through his things. All of his clothes, his mail, his notes, his cabinets, everything, trying to imagine the unimaginable. Of course, I had to figure out how to make it through all of that stuff. Every time, I wouldn't. I liked to go to the mall. Yep, the mall. Retail therapy became my therapy. The temporary high of something new was invigorating to me. For a moment, there was not a care in the world.

On a particular day, my spirit said to me, *What is your next step? You cannot spend your life away, you can't cry the other times, so what are you going to do?* I really began to think about what I was doing and what I needed to do. After all, my dad was not coming back.

I was now being positioned to pivot into another phase of my life. What was that phase? My children were grown. It couldn't be that. Of course, not my dad or other family members. I did have this business I started, and I did have these clients that needed me. Could it be that? I also had this burning desire to make my dad proud of me. I think that is what I am going to do, focus on building my insurance agency.

A year after his passing, we experienced something called COVID-19. It shut the world completely down. You had to stay in the house and could only go out in case of an emergency. My plans had been derailed. Instead of figuring out my pivot, I was trying to figure out how I was going to Target, Walmart, or even Lowe's. That was a bad time. People were losing their loved ones in record numbers. We could not visit family or friends. It was a bad time. I made some really bad choices and decisions during that time. Although they were bad decisions, I think they were the beginning of the actual pivot that I needed to reposition myself in my life and career.

Toward the end of 2020, I started growing my agency with one agent. I was excited, then I became scared, all in the same moments. Now I had real responsibilities to someone other than myself. *Lord, what am I doing? Am I doing the right thing? Well, I did say I wanted to start growing my agency, didn't I? Why am I scared?* These were the many questions I asked myself. It went well. We had a great season that year. He referred another agent to my agency who then referred another. Oh my goodness, now I had five agents.

Lord, what are You doing? I would ask.

The Pivot's True Meaning

Still not understanding exactly what was happening, I embraced it by doing what I do— caring and sharing what I know to help us grow. In 2021, I had an additional three agents to come aboard. How exciting was that? I started thinking again, *Lord, what are you doing? What is happening?* I was growing before my very eyes. Was I really ready for all that He had in store for me? I had all kinds of mixed feelings going on inside. I was not sure I was ready for the large responsibility that had been given to me. I was overcome with fear. But I was up for whatever God was blessing me with. He had been positioning me for a few years, but I had so much going on, I could not see what was in front of me.

At some point, I started seeing a therapist. She was good for my soul. She helped me process life challenges to make me a better person. I also started working with a business coach. Now, I have a therapist for my head and a business coach to help me figure out my business and where I am going with it. They both help me in very different ways yet the exact same ways. I look forward to each meeting with both. I believe they were both very instrumental in helping me to pivot my thoughts of not enough to positioning myself to being more than enough and realizing that I have a thriving agency because God positioned me to pivot through life's highs and lows. I was not sure if my dad was proud of me, they knew he was proud of me. Now I know he was proud of me and would be very proud of where I am and plan on going.

My business coach suggested I study the art of pivoting. There is an art to learning and understanding the true benefits of the pivot. The art of pivoting turned out to be a treasure trove of wisdom. I learned the concept of pivoting as a way to adapt to life's inevitable changes and challenges. Watching videos and reading stories, I realized that my father had been preparing me for this moment all along. No one lives forever, he would say.

As I delved deeper into what I had read and watched, I began to reflect on my own life. I had been making choices and decisions that provided me with little mental stability and kept me feeling unfulfilled. My father had always encouraged me to follow my passions and know that all efforts, including the small ones, will pay off.

Embracing the growth of my insurance agency became the beginning of my journey. I knew that to pivot successfully, I needed to step out of my comfort zone and explore uncharted territories. I value and treasure relationships and experiences more than ever before. Eventually, with every handshake and hug, I embraced my grief and enjoyed the self-discovery of who I am and who I am becoming.

As I began focusing on growing my agency, my agency grew, and opportunities became more available. I began using social media more as a form of advertising. I also repositioned my agency that now we are a part of another agency. This was by far the best decision I had made in years. I traded my retail therapy for growing my business. I know that would have made my dad happy and super proud of me, and this made me happy.

In the midst of my journey, me pivoting to grow my agency and finding focus and purpose has been very therapeutic. It became the perfect tribute to my dad and his legacy of love and guidance, realizing that although he was not here in the flesh, he will always be with me in spirit and forever in my heart.

Meet the Author | Vinara "VEE" Mosby

Vinara Mosby has worked in the insurance industry for more than twenty years. In 2009, she opened her agency, Maxamus Insurance Services, LLC, focusing on the growing mature population in Virginia. Vinara's experience includes enrolling more than six hundred individuals into Medicare Advantage, prescription drug plans, Medicare supplemental plans, life insurance and individual health insurance, as well as dental, vision, and hospital plans. She has also assisted clients with their 401(k) rollovers.

She attributes her agency's growth to consistency, education, and "a love for what we do."

Vinara is the mother of two amazing kids, four grandkids, and one senior dog.

In Vinara's spare time, she loves to travel, bake, and spend time with family and friends.

The Depth of Saying Yes

Ayanna M. Smith

In the realm of life, business, and leadership, the concept of "pivot" holds a multifaceted significance. It embodies the art of adaptability, the courage to change direction, and the resilience to embrace new opportunities. This anthology chapter explores the diverse meanings and profound impact of pivoting in these crucial aspects of our journey. I'm reminded of a few events in my life that truly shifted my thinking and have placed me in a mode to pivot my mindset and that has opened my heart and mind for more.

Saying yes is just the tip of the iceberg. Saying yes has had more depth than I realized. I didn't realize the depth of my yes—when I ultimately said yes to God regarding the things that concerned me and when I said yes to myself, believing that I am going to fully fill up every room that I enter. Own it, don't back down from it, and seek to find more ways to expand in it, then that's when the yes activates the pivot and the pivot translates to a new mind, a new path, and a new alliance to yourself.

Saying Yes to Change and Unexpected Events

Believe that you have everything at your disposal. Whether it's tangible or spiritual, it's on you, in you, and around you. Speaking of tangible things, we are sometimes backed up against the wall with life's valleys. Tragedy can stem from others' hands, our hands, or ultimately God's hands. In this case, I'm reminded of a widow who had two sons. The debt collector came to get monies owed by her deceased husband. Life broadsided this lady. She didn't know what to do. Based on the positioning of the story, the lady's husband didn't have life insurance—yes, let me insert a shameless call to action to make sure all parties, especially the gainfully employed/ breadwinners, don't leave their families in total distress. Side note: It's a travesty to leave the family alone AND a loan to take care of final expenses AND the regular day-to-day expenses. Back to the story...Life just got harder for the widow and her sons. What was she to do now? The creditor was at her door to collect by a certain time or the debt would be settled by having the sons imprisoned.

She clearly didn't realize the depth of the debt her husband owed. She was now filled with grief and seemingly blindsided by the mandatory debt repayment via her sons if the money wasn't produced. She was forced into lack, poverty, loneliness, hopelessness, and utterly frustrated all in one big blow. The lady sought help and counsel through Elisha, a man of God, prophet and spiritual leader in the land.

Elisha asks her, "What do you have in your house?" And she replies, "Your servant has nothing there at all," except a small jar of olive oil. Here's where it gets interesting. Elisha instructs her to go around and borrow as many empty jars as she can from her neighbors. "Don't just get a few," he says, emphasizing the need for abundance in faith and action.

Following Elisha's advice, the widow and her sons start collecting jars and bring them home. Elisha tells her to pour the oil into all the jars, and as she does, something miraculous happens. The oil keeps flowing, filling up one jar after another, until every single jar is brimming. This miraculous event turns her small jar of oil into a vast reserve.

With the jars filled, Elisha advises her to sell the oil, pay off her debts, and live off the rest of the money. This not only solves her immediate financial crisis but also secures her family's future.

A Widow's Story: A Model of Obedience

The story of the widow woman in 2 Kings 4 is a significant narrative in the Bible, which holds several layers of meaning and life lessons. In this story, the widow plays a crucial role in demonstrating obedience and faith in the face of dire circumstances. Let's delve deeper into the significance of her obedience in saying yes:

Trust in the Prophet: The widow's obedience reflects her trust in the prophet Elisha who, as a representative of God, had instructed her to gather empty vessels, and her willingness to follow his guidance demonstrates faith in God's power working through the prophet.

Faith in God's Miraculous Provision: The act of collecting empty pots to pour oil into them may have seemed illogical to many. However, the widow's obedience shows her belief in the possibility of a miracle. She didn't doubt God's ability to provide, even in seemingly impossible situations.

Dependency on God: The widow's situation was dire. She was in debt, her husband had passed away, and creditors were coming to take her sons as slaves. Her obedience signifies her acknowledgment of her helplessness and her decision to rely entirely on God for deliverance. It's a powerful reminder of the importance of dependence on God in times of need.

Multiplication of Resources: The miraculous multiplication of the oil serves as a symbol of God's abundance and provision for those who trust and obey Him. By collecting more pots, the widow actively participated in the process of receiving God's blessings, emphasizing the principle of sowing and reaping.

Community Witness: As the widow gathered the pots and poured the oil, her actions were likely witnessed by her neighbors and community. Her obedience and the subsequent miracle became a powerful testimony to God's faithfulness and might. It could have inspired faith and belief in those who observed the event.

Lesson of Stewardship: The story also teaches us about stewardship. The widow was faithful in collecting the empty vessels, but she was also careful not to waste the oil. This underscores the importance of responsible stewardship of the resources and blessings that God provides.

A Lesson in Surrender: The widow's obedience also illustrates the concept of surrendering to God's will. In her obedience, she surrendered her own plans and expectations to align with God's divine purpose and plan for her life.

Career Pivots

As the widow woman was obedient, I connect that with saying yes to the unknown. As I have walked this life as a professional, I've had to make some decisions that challenged my thinking and led me to the unknown; however, the decisions were for my good. In my career as an educator, I had to pivot and resign from a position that I'd held for a decade. As I sometimes suffer from procrastination and being timely, these two hindrances played into the hands of an unjust and nasty boss. Where the boss should have helped, they found ways to hinder and try to incite a case against me that included me not being fit to serve in that capacity and mandating that I go to a counselor for an evaluation.

Although I could and can work on procrastination and timeliness, being cited as unfit to serve was a personal and destructive attack. If that type of infraction and information was documented on my personnel record, it would greatly damage or end my career. That was not acceptable, but I was grieving the shifts that I had to make regarding this situation. I was scared, angry, and was trying to figure out my next move.

As I shared the accounts leading up to the dramatic end with my mother, she spoke a word that mandated that I pivot and not look back. She told me, "Based on the things you've shared with me and how your boss is handling things, it's not going to turn out right for you. You need to quit the job and trust God!" And as scared as I was, I did just that. I resigned and left what I considered a "good job" and closed that chapter.

Was I hurt? Yes. Was I afraid? Yes. Was I angry? Yes. Did I wish for my boss' downfall? Absolutely. But I had to run like the wind to save my crumbling career and my sanity moreover. I had a real moment where I had to pivot or meet my demise. I went through a few weeks wondering what I was going to do. It's a bit hard to come out of a pattern that was done year after year for over a decade. It was very challenging to recalibrate after such trauma. When all you know is all you know, then it can become crippling to move forward.

Pivot Point: I had to swallow my pride and share what had taken place, generally to a confidant who could potentially help me. It turned out that the person I'd spoken with got me right into another position based on their word. I didn't even interview, but was given a chance to continue my livelihood in the area I'd known for many years. I had to make a decision to say yes and keep moving forward. As the widow woman from the story, I had to "gather my pots" by opening my mouth, so I'd be able to take care of myself.

Pivot Point: I took a position that one may say was a demotion, but with swallowed pride forged ahead anyway. The big takeaway was no one was paying my bills but me, and I was going to hold my head back up one day after feeling like a failure.

Inspiration for Taking Action

At the time of this penning, I've found myself in a few more instances like the widow, having to pivot in mindset. She couldn't see past her current situation, but as aforementioned, she followed instructions, and that led her to not only a better place, but I'd endeavor to say, a wealthy place by having the money to keep her family intact, but also her mind, soul, and spirit. I have had the recent opportunities to be invited to sing and tour internationally. When presented with the opportunity, I immediately said yes without hesitation. I had to then apply for my passport because the last one I had was lost and expired. I took the necessary steps to get that passport process moving. In the midst of passport processing times, I believed that I'd have what I needed before time. And, that's exactly what happened. I have my passport, and now I am ready—as other opportunities arise across the world, I'll be ready to go without hesitation.

Another situation that I said "yes" to was a film festival in my hometown of Bertie County, North Carolina. I went to sing for one segment of the event and ended up auditioning for a screenplay. My yes positioned me to be in the right place at the right time. I only saw a little bit, but the gift that I possess, what I have in my hand, has opened doors. Opportunities to speak are on my list as well and more are coming as I continue to push fear and procrastination aside and trust God. I am ready to push in the area of professional singing, ministry moments and engagements. I am taking the leap to expand in my business like never before, scale it, and move to a new dimension for example with the creation of courses, accepting speaking events to talk about the importance of life insurance and its ability to help people build their portfolios along with offering consulting services for professionals, especially business owners and educators as they advance and develop their gifts.

My yes to the possibilities are massive as mentors and coaches continue to pour into and help me. There are professional women assigned to me who deserve to excel and grow also. They are awaiting my yes. Basically, I have to trust God as a business owner, educator, consultant, vocalist, speaker, and coach to be my catalyst. When I receive instructions, like the widow, to use the oil that I have in my house, gather all of the pots that I have, and even ask others for assistance, then all that's needed will be at my hands.

Questions to Ponder

In the face of unexpected change, it's natural to grapple with fear, uncertainty, and doubt. To navigate these challenges, consider these questions:

1. What must you say yes to? Take a moment to reflect on the changes or challenges in your life. What positive actions or mindset shifts can you say yes to in response to these circumstances?
2. What do you have in your hands that's the solution to your problem? Often, we possess the inner resources and abilities needed to overcome challenges. Identify your strengths and talents, and consider how you can leverage them to navigate change.
3. How will you get through the fear (get uncomfortable) to do what's being asked? Fear is a natural response to change, but it doesn't have to paralyze you. Embrace discomfort as a sign

of growth, and take small, intentional steps toward your
goals.

Please note the significance of the widow woman's obedience in
gathering the pots for the oil because it lies in her unwavering trust in
God's power and provision, her willingness to act on faith and the
powerful demonstration of God's miraculous blessings in response to
her obedience. This story serves as an inspiration for all to trust God
even in challenging circumstances and to act in obedience to His
guidance. Go from saying "this is all we have" to seeing it as the
answer to all we need. Believe that you have everything at your
disposal. Whether it's tangible or spiritual, it's on you, in you, and
around you.

Speaking of tangible things, life has a way of throwing unexpected
challenges our way. These unexpected events can often feel like a
storm crashing upon us, leaving us bewildered and disoriented, yet
it's during these very moments of upheaval that the power of saying
yes to change becomes most evident.

The widow was thrust into a dire situation, one that she could not
have anticipated or prepared for. The sudden death of her husband,
coupled with the looming debt and the threat of her sons being taken
away, pushed her to the brink of despair. In the face of such adversity,
she had a choice: to succumb to the weight of her circumstances or to
say "yes" to the possibility of change.

It's in moments like these that we're reminded of the incredible
strength of the human spirit. When we say yes to change, we're
essentially saying yes to resilience, adaptability, and the unwavering
belief that, even in our darkest hours, there's a glimmer of hope. This
choice is not just about acknowledging the existence of change but
embracing it as an opportunity for growth.

Meet the Author | Ayanna M. Smith

Ayanna M. Smith, the chief executive officer of A. M. Smith & Company LLC, emerges as a beacon of authority and inspiration, especially for professional and entrepreneurial women seeking financial mastery.

With a remarkable background steeped in the world of finance, Ayanna shines as a revered life insurance broker, a prolific four-time published author, a motivational speaker, a dedicated coach, an adept facilitator, and an indomitable lifelong educator. Her journey reflects a commitment that runs deep, inspired by a lineage of esteemed educators.

Her captivating leadership spans both classroom and administrative domains, resonating effortlessly with scholars and mentors alike. In the realm of finance, Ayanna's passion takes flight as an advocate, empowering individuals and families to navigate their financial outlook. Her dedication to bridging the gap in historically marginalized communities through conversations about "generational wealth and health" is unwavering, evident in her establishment of a financial literacy sanctuary in Portsmouth, Virginia, in February 2022.

Ayanna M. Smith

Ayanna's prowess radiates across esteemed platforms where she imparts financial counsel, equipping captivated audiences with invaluable tools. Witness her brilliance firsthand on *Money Talks with Ayanna Smith,* her engaging weekly livestream show.

A distinguished alumna of North Carolina Central University with a foundation in elementary education, Ayanna's academic journey extended to Regent University, where she specialized in educational leadership. Her unquenchable thirst for knowledge led her to embark on doctoral studies in organizational leadership at Nova Southeastern University—a testament to her dedication to personal and collective growth.

Ayanna stands as an exemplary and authoritative figure, guiding women toward financial elevation. For those seeking empowerment and a roadmap to prosperity, Ayanna's transformative journey is a beacon of inspiration. In addition to Ayanna's love for sharing financial literacy and life insurance strategies, Ayanna is a professional singer, coach, and speaker.

Ayanna may be contacted via email at amsmith.companyllc@gmail.com or by visiting www.ayannamsmith.com.

Unleash Your Potential

A Journey of Pivot Aligned with Passion, Purpose, and Potential

Dr. Valarie Williams Harris

Have you ever felt the electric surge of excitement from standing at the peak of something extraordinary? Imagine a life where every day is a canvas, and you are the artist, ready to paint your masterpiece. This is the thrill awaiting you as you embark on a journey of transformation—a journey where you will learn to position yourself to pivot, not merely for change's sake, but in a way that aligns with your core values, passion, purpose, potential, and goals.

Picture this: Your core values are your North Star, your unwavering guide, ensuring that every step you take is in harmony with your deepest convictions. Your passion fuels your journey with a relentless fire, making every challenge an adventure and every endeavor a labor of love. Your purpose is the lighthouse that shines brightly in the darkest times, guiding you toward a more significant meaning in everything you do. Your potential is a treasure chest waiting to be unlocked, filled with possibilities you have yet to discover. And your goals are the milestones that lead you to the life you have always dreamed of.

Imagine unleashing all this in a symphony of personal growth, where change is not a daunting unknown but an exhilarating opportunity to become the best version of yourself. This is the journey we are about to embark upon, and it is like no other. In my personal life, I have taken audacious steps to pivot alongside the ever-evolving trends of technology. I have remained open to acquiring diverse knowledge and skills, all with the purpose of being well-prepared to assist others in doing the same.

So, fasten your seatbelt, dear reader, because we are diving into a world where pivoting is not just a strategic move but a transformational experience. Are you ready to eliminate the fear of change and step into unlimited potential? Are you prepared to position yourself to pivot, soar higher, and embrace the greatness within you? If your answer is a resounding yes, then get ready to unlock your potential, chase your passion, and live a life that is authentically yours, filled with purpose, and driven by your loftiest goals. The adventure begins now.

Recognize the Need for Change in Your Personal Life

From my teenage years—1966 to now at the age of seventy—I wrestled with stifling weight, not just around my waistline but also on my soul. As I talk about this, it clearly reminds me that I was entangled in a vicious cycle, indulging in unhealthy eating habits, only to be reprimanded by a myriad of health conditions—high blood pressure, diabetes, sleep apnea. You name it, I had it. A cocktail of medication and medical advice couldn't illuminate my foggy mind or infuse energy into my lethargic limbs. In essence, I was the architect of my own demise. But a voice within whispered, "You have greatness inside of you that the world needs." I knew that reclaiming my life would require a monumental shift—a true pivotal moment.

It was when I found myself, cane in hand and unexplained weakness, that the lightbulb finally flickered on. I realized this had to stop.

Something had to give. Inspired by Oprah, who once said, "You do not become what you want; you become what you believe," I knew it was time for a U-turn—a complete overhaul of my lifestyle.

So, I took the leap. I embraced exercise, only to stumble again; the scale didn't budge. Why? Because I was still shackled by my poor eating habits. It was at this point that I took another gigantic step: joining Weight Watchers. Fast forward, and fifty pounds lighter, I was a new person—but the transformation wasn't merely physical. It was spiritual, emotional, holistic.

According to both the Centers for Disease Control and Prevention and the World Health Organization, I was far from alone in my struggle. Millions are lost in the labyrinth of obesity, with its mazelike turns of health issues and diminished quality of life. If you are on this journey, my message to you is simple: Empower yourself to change. Your health is your wealth; invest in it like you would a cherished treasure.

Every day became an exercise in self-love and self-discipline. I began eating balanced meals, hydrating generously, and resting adequately. Let me tell you, it wasn't a stroll in the park, yet I had to remain steadfast, fueling my perseverance through both prayer and action.

Even today, as a wife, mother, entrepreneur, and educator, the old triggers and stressors hover like uninvited guests at a party. Hence, in my profession, I never underestimate the value of a healthy lifestyle. You can't truly lead or achieve your potential if you're weighed down literally by poor health.

My challenge to you? Take the reins of your health journey. Rejuvenate your mindset daily. After all, as the saying goes, "If you think wellness is expensive, try illness."

Fast forward to 2016, and the specter of my old self reappeared. Yes, despite my earlier transformation, I found myself entangled with obesity once again. Ah, the struggle is real, but you see, every challenge is a stepping stone to a better you. I looked in the mirror and saw the eyes of someone who was weary but not defeated. In that pivotal moment, I whispered to myself, "Not again. This ends now."

And so, another chapter began. This time, the weight loss totaled an astounding ninety pounds.

I took the wise words of Nelson Mandela to heart: "I am the master of my fate; I am the captain of my soul." Not only did the pounds melt away, but so did my high blood pressure, sleep apnea, and diabetes. They dissolved, like morning mist under the blaze of a new dawn.

My relationship with food had to be rewritten, as if it were a script from a play that no longer served me. Every bite became an exercise in mindfulness, every meal a strategic plan of nourishment. I learned to be on high alert, savoring my food but also recognizing when to put down the fork. I trained myself to listen to the whispers of my body, rather than the loud disharmony of temptation.

Today, I stand before you, and obesity no longer casts its daunting shadow over my life. If I, with all my previous pitfalls, could orchestrate such a turnaround, then believe me, so can you.

Challenge yourself today. Whether you aim to lose weight, build a business, or achieve academic excellence, the core principle remains the same—empower yourself to take control. Reaffirm daily: *Obesity will not have its way in my life. I have greatness inside of me that the world needs.* The ball is in your court. You have the tools; now forge your path. If I can do it, trust me, so can you.

It is delightful to have the opportunity to engage and embark on a journey of personal growth and transformation. In this chapter, my focus revolves around the profound concept of being positioned to pivot. It is only after embracing the pivot that one begins to change, grow, and transform. Remember this positioning to pivot is not a one-time occasion in one's life. It is ongoing, but you must be willing to trust the turns in life you will have to take.

Embrace Professional Challenges with a New Mindset

In life, often we might find ourselves in a state of complacency, where feelings of unfulfillment, self-doubt, and a sense of insignificance can prevail. It's a place where procrastination and a belief in unnoticed potential can take root. Over the course of my thirty-four-year career as an educator and twenty-five years as an entrepreneur, I, too, encountered these sentiments. I was ensnared in a place of contentment without even realizing it.

When I began to finally embrace the profound truth within myself, then I began to realize the incredible power to chart a new course, reshape my vocation, and navigate toward the life I truly desired. It is vital that you recognize that you have the unwavering ability to change your direction and forge a future that reflects your deepest aspirations.

It is not uncommon to encounter personal and professional challenges at various points in life. During a period in my life, I experienced stagnation, health concerns, and unfulfilled dreams that were profoundly disheartening. However, these challenges served as powerful catalysts for change and personal growth in my life.

In moments of stagnation, it is essential to recognize that you possess the inner power to pivot and embrace a new pathway. Unfulfilled dreams can be rekindled, health concerns can lead to a focus on self-care, and feelings of unfulfillment can drive you toward more purposeful endeavors. Your journey is a dynamic one, filled with opportunities to pivot and craft a life that aligns more closely with your core values and aspirations.

Yet, through introspection and self-assessment, I unearthed my genuine passion and purpose. I wholeheartedly embraced my passion and assumed a new role as a certified life empowerment coach and business consultant. This transformation empowered me to serve and uplift others in their quest to discover their worth and their own positioning to pivot.

Throughout my journey, I came to appreciate the significance of honing in more on prayer, passion, purpose, preparation, persistence, and a positive mindset, what I refer to as my Six P Core Principles. These principles guided me in repositioning myself and effectively navigating the challenges that arose.

Positioning oneself to pivot is a personal journey, and the contours of everyone's comfort zone differs. Patience is required, along with the celebration of even the smallest victories along the way. Embrace your passion, foster self-belief, and recognize the greatness within you that the world eagerly awaits.

Remember that your experiences, even the most challenging ones, can be the stepping stones to a more meaningful and fulfilling future. They provide valuable insights and motivation for positive change. Our experiences in life have been shown to be our best teaching moments.

Embracing the Uncomfortable

Let's talk about the captivating force of storytelling. This craft has been instrumental in my journey, both as a leader and as an author. Through weaving the threads of my own experiences into relatable narratives, I have connected deeply with my audience, inspiring them to face their own challenges and seek transformation. As I established myself in the publishing realm, it was not just another title added to my name. It was a significant pivot, enabling me not only to publish my own books but also to empower others to share their own stories.

Take a moment with me and listen to this deeply personal chapter in my life. I was once called a "moron" by a teacher, a crushing insult hurled in front of an entire classroom. That experience could have broken me, but instead, it fueled a relentless drive. I pivoted, propelled by a determination to rise above that degradation and oh, how I soared.

And it is not just my journey. I see this transformative potential daily in those I coach. Take one of my clients, an extraordinary talent bogged down by self-doubt. Through our coaching partnership, she unleashed her true potential, pivoting into an awe-inspiring trajectory. She launched her own business, penned books, and even crafted training modules to disperse her wisdom. Her story is yet another testament to the boundless opportunities that emerge when we position ourselves to make that all-important pivot.

So, you see, whether it is through the eloquence of storytelling, surmounting personal obstacles, or catalyzing change in others, the essence is always the same—the power to pivot is within us all. Are you ready to unlock yours?

Say it out loud: "I have greatness inside of me that the world needs." Embrace it. Now it is time to channel that innate greatness into using your skills as a catalyst for change. Even at the age of seventy, I still leap out of my comfort zone into tech-empowered efforts so that I can assist others who don't understand new concepts that will enable them to embrace their individual capacity, which many times brings about a rewarding and life-changing experience.

As you make strategic pivots, unleashing your technological powers becomes vital, irrespective of your business or personal aspirations, for it opens the door to boundless opportunities. When I begin to think about it that way, it is an electrifying time to be alive. We are standing at the crossroads of change and opportunity, and at the heart of it all lies the captivating power of new trends in technology. It is as if we are holding the keys to a treasure chest full of possibilities, and all we need to do is unlock it. As the legendary Steve Jobs once said, "Technology is nothing. What's important is that you have faith in people, that they are good and smart, and if you give them tools, they'll do wonderful things with them."

This brings me to my own personal odyssey into the digital frontier. Let me take you down memory lane. When I first stepped into the field of education, chalk and blackboard were the stars of the classroom. Fast forward to today, and we are navigating virtual classrooms, computer-driven curriculum, and gamified learning experiences. Technology has allowed us to transcend geographical boundaries, enriching lives all over the world. My work with the missions team for Global Missions in Ghana was significantly augmented through technology, furthering the reach and impact of our humanitarian endeavors.

In my life journey, I have experienced the transformative impact of what I call the Four Pillars of Technological Empowerment. Each of these pillars serves as a guidepost for me, illustrating how to channel the immense power of technology to uplift not just your own life, but also the lives of those around you.

1. **Digital Literacy:** Start by gaining a basic understanding of the digital landscape. Platforms like Microsoft offer courses to arm you with this essential skillset.
2. **Networking:** Social media isn't just for sharing news; it is a powerful tool for connecting with like-minded individuals, thought leaders, and mentors.
3. **Lifelong Learning:** The digital realm is ever evolving. Keep up with the latest trends and technologies by committing to continuous learning.
4. **Innovation:** Got an idea? Technology can help you turn that concept into a reality. Explore platforms like Kickstarter and IndieGoGo to find support for your vision and new ideas.

Unleash Your Potential

Friends, the technology train is leaving the station, and you do not want to be left behind. Dive headfirst into this new realm of opportunities. Take that online course, connect with a mentor, and launch your dream project. It is time to marry your innate brilliance with the tools that can amplify it to unprecedented levels.

There is a whole world waiting to be transformed by you, so go on, unleash the power of technology, and become the change you want to see. Your destiny awaits, and it is one click away. Embrace the journey, you trailblazer! As we journey through the maze of life's opportunities, one tool stands out as a constant catalyst for transformation: technology. As we all know, "The best way to predict the future is to invent it," a pearl of wisdom from Alan Kay, a computer science pioneer.

Your positioning matters when it comes to understanding your unique strengths and goals. It is pivotal when leveraging technology awareness. Are you an educator like me looking to reshape the learning experience, or are you an aspiring entrepreneur with a vision to disrupt the market? Wherever you stand, your position defines your pivot.

There are a few principles that can serve as a guiding light to illuminate your tech-empowered path:

1. **Self-assessment:** Start by understanding your current skills and how they align with your goals. This is your baseline, your starting position.
2. **Focus on Adaptability:** Technology is a fast-paced field. Your ability to adapt to new tools and trends could be your greatest asset.

3. **Data-Driven Decisions:** Utilize analytics and data to assess the impact of your tech initiatives. The insights will guide your next pivot.

Challenges Will Bring About Positivity in Your Life

The transformative power of pivoting is amazing. Let me recount my odyssey in the intricate world of social media, a realm that I only started to navigate in 2017. Picture a timid social media newbie, scattering a *like* or a *love* like rare gems, yet never diving deep into the sea of digital interactions. Yes, that was me.

What sparked my pivot? It was a bold challenge to go live on Facebook for six weeks. Just the mere thought of it sent chills down my spine, yet it was this exact leap out of my comfort zone that tossed me into a whole new stratosphere.

Remember, it is not about the resources, but your resourcefulness. Embrace the positivity and tune out the negativity that often comes hand-in-hand with social media. Since that challenge, I have put on multiple hats—I host my own show, maintain my website, and coach and consult with clients. You will see my digital footprint from Instagram to LinkedIn, Facebook to my very own YouTube channel. Now that is a pivot!

A renown author that I respect, John C. Maxwell, said, "Change is inevitable. Growth is optional." The pivot wasn't just a change. It was a metamorphosis, an evolution, a journey from cocoon to butterfly. So, if you ever find yourself standing at the crossroads of change, remember: Positioning yourself to pivot is not just advisable, it is essential.

So, are you ready to make your pivot? Whether it is in your personal development, career, or social media engagement, the time to pivot is now. Go on, make your U-turn. Your new direction awaits.

I do believe my story is the embodiment of many remarkable U-turns that transformed me from a social media novice into a multifaceted influencer. If that is not empowerment, I don't know what is. In my incredible journey, I've navigated diverse terrains—personal growth, professional excellence, health, wellness, and entrepreneurial ventures. In the realm of health, let me tell you, the struggle was real. But I flipped the script, triumphed over obesity, and regained my well-being. I went from being constrained by numerous health issues to liberating myself, losing ninety pounds, and saying goodbye to medications. If that is not personal empowerment materializing as physical transformation, I don't know what is.

Professionally speaking, my dedication to education has enriched the lives of educators, women leaders, and budding entrepreneurs. As a certified empowerment coach and business consultant, I have unlocked the gates of wisdom and leadership, not just for myself but for countless others. Don't forget, I also have an academic arsenal that features multiple degrees, reflecting my status as a lifelong learner.

Wow. Let's talk about social media. The platform I initially tiptoed around has now become a stage where I shine. I took the bull by the horns, and today, I am not just posting, I'm hosting—my own show, that is. Plus, consulting, coaching, and running my own business, emphasizing the importance of health and wellness in achieving professional milestones.

So, what's the golden thread that ties all these aspects together? The ability to pivot. Whether it is turning my health around, scaling professional heights, or embracing the digital age, my life is a testament to the power of making that pivotal U-turn when it matters the most.

In essence, I'm living proof that transformation is not confined to one area of life. We all have the potential for incredible change and growth. All we need to do is position ourselves to pivot. So, are you ready to make your turn? I have made mine, and the view from here is spectacular. My canvas is still in progress. What a beautiful sight to see. Age is only a number, and if we can think, move, see, hear all the essentials, there is work that needs to be done in the earth. You have what it takes to make the pivot ...people are waiting on you.

As I conclude this chapter, the reason I do what I do today is because of an illustrious career spanning over four decades in education, leadership, and personal development. I ventured into entrepreneurship to actualize a vision that transcends the traditional boundaries of these fields. My journey as a small business owner began as an extension of my lifelong commitment to empowerment and transformation. After years of coaching and consulting, I recognized a gaping need for a specialized firm that could serve as a hub for personal and professional development.

This realization led to the birth of the Stepping Up and Stepping Out Coaching Academy—a sanctuary for individuals and organizations seeking meaningful change and unparalleled growth. The academy is a culmination of my extensive experience, channeling it into actionable pathways that empower others to achieve their fullest potential. My academic background, enriched by degrees from Norfolk State University, Virginia Tech University, Liberty University, and a doctoral degree from Seraphim Ministries International Bible College, provides a well-rounded foundation for this venture.

My business is also a manifestation of my global perspective and unwavering dedication to humanitarian causes, having been involved in missions in Ghana and disaster relief efforts in Grenada. I realized that the principles I had been teaching in various global settings could be systematized and offered to a broader audience through a formalized platform.

Becoming a small business owner was not just a career move; it was a calling—an opportunity to amplify my impact and leave an indelible mark on the lives of those aspiring for greatness. Every coaching session, every workshop, and every piece of advice dispensed through my academy is a step toward fulfilling this higher purpose. I am not merely in the business of coaching; I am in the business of transformation. And in doing so, I have found my ultimate life's work.

Embracing your passion will give you the drive, new mind shift, and motivation to leave a legacy that will positively impact future generations. Imagine having the confidence to pursue your passion while unlocking your hidden potential to step out with purpose.

Meet the Author | Dr. Valarie Williams Harris

As a retired educator, minister, director of ministries, author, speaker, certified empowerment coach and business consultant, Valarie utilizes forty-plus years of experience helping educators, leaders, women in leadership, and entrepreneurs develop clarity to achieve their goals by cultivating a brand that offers the necessary tools, resources, strategic planning, and training so they can succeed in their personal and professional development.

Valarie has a B.S. degree from Norfolk State University, a master's degree from Virginia Tech University and Seraphim Ministries International Bible College, a worship studies degree from Liberty University, and a doctoral degree from Seraphim Ministries International Bible College. She has traveled with the Uniquely Chosen Hope Missions Team for Global Missions in Ghana, West Africa, in May 2017, 2018, 2019, and 2023. She has also traveled to Mumbai, India, Alaska, Puerto Rico, Amsterdam, London, Brussels, Paris, and the Western and the Eastern Caribbean. In May 2022, Valarie spent ten days in the island nation of Grenada working with the Share Hope International Ministries team on a disaster relief project.

As a minister, she has a heart for those who desire a closer spiritual walk with God. Her purpose is to glorify God in everything she does. She cherishes her life with her husband, Shurman Harris; their two daughters, Stacey M. Robinson and Tia M. Jones; five grandchildren; and four great-grandchildren who are the loves of her life.

Valarie is a small business owner of the Stepping Out with Purpose, LLC Coaching & Consulting Company. She believes embracing your passion will give you the drive, new mind shift, and motivation to ensure success in unlocking your hidden potential to step out with purpose. She works diligently with her clients to help them build a business that will create financial freedom and a healthy lifestyle to leave a legacy that will positively impact future generations.

Valarie is the author of eight books, including *Talk Time with God, Unleashed Power of Prayer Teens and Young Adults' Prayer Journal Workbook, Stepping Up & Stepping Out Journaling Experience,* and *The Effect of Prayer in the Life of a Leader.* She is a co-author of *PEARLS* and *Positioned to Pivot,* the visionary author of *Influencers Stepping Out in Boldness* and a new book that will be released in 2024, *Stepping Beyond Your Comfort Zone.*

Read more: www.steppingoutwithpurpose.com.

The Ultimate Comeback—Get Back in the Game

Dr. Tabatha Spurlock

An Educational Foundation

In the early 1990s, I was a student residing in Chester, Virginia. My passion lay in singing in chorus classes throughout my middle school years, cherishing each grade level and every course. We performed at school concerts, community events, and even journeyed across the Chesterfield County school district for competitions. However, as my eighth-grade year drew to a close, the excitement was about to fade.

I vividly recall sitting down with my counselor to explore elective courses for high school, and in that transformative moment, a life-altering realization dawned upon me. While I possessed the ability to hit the high notes as a soprano, I harbored no aspirations of pursuing a professional singing career. Consequently, I made the decision to embark on a path focused on business courses for my high school education.

In my senior year at Thomas Dale High School, I had the privilege of being a cooperative office education (COE) student. This unique program divided my day, with half spent at school and the other half dedicated to work. My placement was at a company known as Philip Morris, and it marked my introduction to the world of corporate America. This invaluable work experience sparked a deep interest in pursuing a career, either within the same industry or within the federal government. At that point in life, I didn't have many connections in either of those spheres, but my formative years in school taught me one crucial lesson: Both sectors offered the potential for a stable and comfortable financial future, and I was eager to be a part of it. A few of the relationships formed with colleagues and mentors would last another twenty years.

During my journey toward a future in business, there's a memorable moment that stands out in my mind relative to my current entrepreneurship. I recall composing a poem as part of a class assignment. Although I occasionally dabbled in writing poems for my own enjoyment as a teenager, this particular instance offered me the opportunity to become a published author. My teacher collected the poems created by my classmates and me, and she compiled them into a book. While I can't recall the book's name or the title of my specific poem, one thing I do remember is gifting the book to my mother as a cherished keepsake.

I didn't fully grasp the significance of being a published author at the time. I was unaware of the admiration and respect that often accompanies such a career choice, and I certainly never envisioned it as a part of my future. It wasn't until about two decades later that I would unexpectedly embark on the entrepreneurial journey of becoming a published author again. This was a path that had never been on my childhood list of aspirations, but it would eventually become a significant venture in my adulthood.

Moment of Reflection: Take a few moments to think about your high school self and those aspirations you wrote in your yearbook. Did you pursue the same career field, or have your skills and talents led you into another sector?

A Grassroots Beginning

With an illustrious career spanning nearly two decades, I'm humble to be deemed as a beacon of educational leadership, community involvement, and unwavering resilience. My journey has been a testament to the power of dedication, passion, and an undying commitment to fostering growth and empowerment in the lives of many. During the latter two years of completing my undergraduate degree in business administration and management on a small business/entrepreneurship track from Virginia Commonwealth University, I began to work part-time at a local Boys & Girls Clubs in a low-income neighborhood. It was important for me to give back in a way that I had never imagined. My childhood aspiration of securing a stable career with the federal government or corporate America was slowly diminishing into a life of service.

This early experience laid the foundation for my values and vision, anchoring a belief in the potential every child possesses, irrespective of their background. Fortunately, I was driven by my humble beginnings, having been raised in a low-income neighborhood yet surrounded by love in the home. Every day that I went to work, I could relate to the struggles of the parents and the wants and desires of the kids in those underserved communities. They were people with big, loving, and caring hearts who wanted more out of life than the poverty- and crime-stricken neighborhood in which they resided. With a little exposure and the right mentors, they could truly be anything they wanted to be in life.

Moment of Reflection: Take a moment to reflect on the onset of your professional career. Who was instrumental as a leader or mentor to help propel your career? What lessons do you recall from then that still apply to your life now?

Rising Through the Ranks

My dedication to education wasn't limited to community outreach. Over the years, I've fulfilled multiple roles within the public K–12 education system that were indicative of my educational and professional backgrounds. From starting in the classroom environment as a career-switching business teacher, I transitioned seamlessly into multiple significant positions at the district level, each role reinforcing my commitment to making quality education accessible to all.

As the inaugural career and technical education (CTE) academic advisor for an inner-city district, I now stand as the nexus of education and community engagement. In this pivotal role, I tirelessly bridge the gap between academia and real-world career pathways, ensuring students are not only educated but also prepared for their future. By fostering community partnerships, I am able to help foster relationships and experiences among secondary students and professionals in the community.

Besides a passion for business and education, I too enjoy conducting research. My academic pursuits have been nothing short of groundbreaking. My dissertation, focused on e-mentoring practices in school-based mentoring programs, is a pioneering piece of research in the field. This research isn't just theoretical for me, and I embrace opportunities where I can translate my findings into actionable and life-changing strategies. I actively support mentoring efforts as a board member for the nonprofit MEGA Mentors, and I'm headed into my second two-year term.

My expertise hasn't gone unnoticed from recognition with numerous educational awards and presenting at conferences and events on various scales—state, regional, and national. I haven't confined my impact to schools and colleges. I perform philanthropic work and have a heart for community development. Being involved with multiple community organizations strongly supports my belief in collective growth. Whether it's through mentorship, community service, or philanthropic endeavors, I've made it my mission to uplift, motivate, and inspire others around me.

> *Moment of Reflection: Take a moment to list all of the ways you currently give back to others and your community. Who are your community partners? What skills have you mastered to support you with your service-based endeavors?*

Life-Altering Season

The year 2016 marked a pivotal moment in my life when I endured a traumatic accident that put my spirit, resilience, and faith to the test. I emerged from this adversity not only stronger, but also more determined with a deeper sense of purpose. My personal journey of recovery has since become a wellspring of inspiration for numerous individuals. The transformative experience led me to establish my current venture, Empower One, Inspire Many, in 2017 and later propelled me to achieve the status of a best-selling children's book author in 2020. My journey didn't stop there, as in 2022, I further expanded my business to encompass a women's empowerment initiative called Let's Wine About It.

Before we celebrate my comeback, I believe it's crucial to provide you with insight into the journey I undertook to survive such a traumatic experience. I aim to walk you through the steps I traversed, one at a time, because walking away from my dream job was a bittersweet decision. At the time, I believed I had reached a pinnacle in my career as a district leader promoting mentoring. However, life took an unexpected turn as I grappled with the diagnoses of post-traumatic stress disorder, anxiety, and depression, all while navigating this new reality with limited support systems in place. Before I knew it, I found myself overwhelmed and decided to take a step back to regain control of my life.

Over the next two years, I dedicated myself to completing my doctoral program while also engaging in consulting and part-time teaching. Yet, the burden of medical expenses from out-of-pocket coverage became increasingly challenging to manage. This served as a clear signal that it was time for me to reenter the workforce on a full-time basis. Interestingly, this decision coincided with the onset of the 2020 global pandemic, further adding to the complexity of my journey. I began to journal as a way to cope, and I'm blessed to become a serial best-selling author of a children's book and several empowerment books.

> *Moment of Reflection: What's a major setback you've had to encounter that altered your way of living? How did the setback interfere with your personal and professional goals?*

The Comeback

By now, you've read quite a bit about the onset of my career and life-altering experiences. I transparently shared my setbacks and successes as a way to encourage you to get back in the game. I want you to know that you're not alone. I was able to use the strategies I'm about to share to secure my current position. Here are seven steps that helped me return to the workforce full-time and reclaim a better leadership position than the one I humbly resigned from back in 2017.

No. 1 - Take time to heal.

My traumatic accident from 2016 took a major toll on me physically, emotionally, and mentally. I honestly didn't know how to adjust from being a natural go-getter to moving, literally and figuratively, at a slower pace in life. As I look back and reflect on those moments, I can't help but say "Lord, I thank You" for delivering me from the pain and setbacks. The journey to "getting back in the game" was not easy by far. There were personal and professional hurdles I had to conquer.

Personally, I had to let some people and things go. It was disheartening yet eye-opening that I had to learn how to love some people from afar or cut the toxic relationship off altogether. Professionally, it took twenty-eight months for me to gain the courage to return to full-time employment. Was I scared? Did I have reservations about the transition from part-time employment? Absolutely! However, my fear of poverty was greater than my fear of change. I had to remind myself of my work-related and entrepreneurial efforts during my hiatus. I put in the work and understood how to embrace self-care strategies, particularly ways to lower my anxiety and manage the depression.

You may not be fully healed, but you're healed enough to get back on the playing field. I didn't trust myself to jump back into a leadership position where I had to directly or indirectly supervise others; however, I felt confident and comfortable enough to lead students in a classroom. It took quite a bit of preparation with counseling, journaling, healthy periods of isolation, physical therapy, and prayer.

Moment of Reflection: Ask yourself: What or who am I holding on to that I need to let go of in order to properly heal to get to my next level in life?

No. 2 - Take time for a self-assessment of your skills and talents.

Make a list of your skills, strengths, areas of growth, likes, and dislikes. You have been out of the game for some time, so it's important to honestly reflect on a path of interest and passion. Don't overthink this strategy. Simply take out a piece of paper, find a pen or pencil, and write out your list. You can also use a phone or a tablet to make your list. Be kind to yourself, and give yourself some grace. If you've identified any gaps in your skills or knowledge, now is a great time to address them. Take online courses, attend workshops or webinars, and even consider getting a certification in your field.

When I created my list, being a classroom teacher was at the top. During my hiatus, I also invested in professional development opportunities by attending webinars, watching motivational and inspirational YouTube videos, and reading articles. Don't sit on your gifts and talents while you wait to get back in the game.

Moment of Reflection: What have you done or plan to do to help you stay relevant and current with your skills and talents?

No. 3 - Update your résumé.

Ensure your résumé is up to date, encompassing all pertinent work experience, skills, and achievements. Don't forget to emphasize any volunteer work, freelance projects, online courses, or webinars you've completed during your time away from the workforce. As you revise your résumé on platforms like Google Docs or Microsoft Word, remember to keep your virtual résumé on LinkedIn current as well.

In today's society, LinkedIn is an invaluable tool. Actively engage with the platform by selecting your preferred career fields, which can lead to receiving emails about potential job opportunities. While I opted for a familiar position for a seamless transition, you might consider venturing into a new field. LinkedIn serves as an effective means to network with professionals in your industry, connect with job seekers and recruiters, and showcase your professional portfolio. Given that you've already compiled a list of your skills, strengths, and accomplishments, use this information to enhance your credibility and establish a robust personal brand.

Moment of Reflection: Do you need to supplement your résumé with additional skills and completed tasks to align it better with your goals?

No. 4 - Networking, Networking, and More Networking

While attending local events, take the opportunity to inquire with both new and old friends about potential job openings within their companies. It's entirely reasonable to express your interest in exploring new career opportunities and keeping your options open. You may also have maintained connections with former colleagues and mentors. When engaging with former colleagues, be upfront about your desire to re-enter the workforce and your enthusiasm for the possibility of working together once again.

As for your mentors, seek their assistance in brainstorming potential job prospects within your current field. Sometimes, our own plans can inadvertently limit our thinking regarding personal growth opportunities. A trusted, caring, and candid mentor can be a valuable resource in guiding you in the right direction. Your mentors could even be members from social and professional organizations.

Moment of Reflection: Make a list of individuals who can help you with career advancement.

No. 5 - Apply for multiple positions.

Utilize your freshly updated résumé as a foundation to tailor your application for the positions you aspire to attain. Don't hesitate to reach for roles that align with your qualifications and ambitions, even if you don't meet every single requirement listed in the job description. Remember that on-the-job training exists for a purpose, and you can bridge any skill gaps as you progress.

By stepping into new roles, you'll have the opportunity to introduce innovative ideas that could lead to a positive cultural transformation. Grant yourself permission to evolve and reach new heights in your career. To broaden my horizons and explore fresh opportunities, I applied for positions within different school districts forty-five miles apart.

Moment of Reflection: Create a spreadsheet of the positions you plan to apply for, company description, and document follow-up conversations leading to a job offer.

No. 6 - Show Up for Yourself.

Dedicate time to rehearsing responses to typical interview questions and be prepared to address any gaps in your full-time employment history with confidence. It's crucial to thoroughly research the company beforehand anticipating potential questions that may arise during the interview. Tailoring your responses to align with the specific company's values and expectations is a timeless practice. Staying current with the evolving skillsets employers may seek is vital. Striking a balance between work and life is also of utmost importance in today's job market.

When you receive a call or email about a job interview, trust the process. Give yourself room for options with multiple offers. Prepare your outfit meticulously, and be prepared to make a lasting impression on the panel interview or with the interviewer. Take a moment to acknowledge and celebrate your journey—your resilience, self-reflection, and determination.

Moment of Reflection: Ask yourself, Am I really ready? *Call a family member or friend to help you prepare and reassure you that you're ready, if needed.*

No. 7 - Congratulations! You Got the Job!

You did it! You got the job! Select the best start date and slowly get your rhythm back of working full-time again. I know you're going to give one hundred percent, but don't exhaust and push yourself too much too soon. You've already proven you can do the job in the interview. Give yourself time to deliver with daily effort. You are your only competition and only have something to prove to yourself. You're transitioning from survival mode to being a boss again. Stay positive knowing that your setbacks were only setups for your ultimate comeback. What you thought you lost during your part-time season, God will replace and make it ten times better. I am a witness!

Moment of Reflection: How do you plan to celebrate your big win?

Remember, everyone's journey back into the workforce will be unique, so adjust these steps as necessary to fit your situation. In the words of Sha'Carri Richardson, the world's fastest woman, "I'm not back. I'm better!" I wish you nothing but the best as you get back in the game!

Meet the Author | Dr. Tabatha Spurlock

Dr. Tabatha Spurlock is an author, motivational speaker, and esteemed educational leader with two decades of experience. A celebrated philanthropist, author, and Top 40 Under 40 awardee, her research in e-mentoring and her innovative B.O.S.S. method from her empowerment company have garnered acclaim. Her storytelling prowess has further been solidified through her endeavors as a serial bestselling author. By sharing her story, she offers a beacon of hope to others navigating their own challenges, reminding them of the power of perseverance and the importance of community. A resilient advocate, her passion illuminates her commitment to youth. While she enjoys her educational and community pursuits, her number one priority and passion in life is being a mom to her daughter, Kennedi.

About the Company

Empower One, Inspire Many LLC is a life empowerment company with multifaceted endeavors. We help thriving women and mothers bounce back from life's setbacks through a signature coaching program called B.O.S.S., the Let's Wine About It mastermind and events, and empower youth with bestselling children's book and curriculum, A Promise is a Promise. Find out more at www.empower1inspiremany.com.

The Platform Builder

Build Your Personal Brand in the Workplace to Increase Your Morale and Own Your Career Destiny

Sharvette Mitchell

Guess what? Just as Apple inspired many to "Think Different" or how Nike rallied us all to "Just Do It," there's immense power in a brand's message. Do you remember the commercial, "Red Bull gives you wings"? These iconic phrases weren't just catchy slogans. They became the soul of their companies, encapsulating their essence and vision. Why is this important you may ask? Here's why: They represent not only the magic of branding but also the heart and values of an organization. As Dr. Sean Gresh, from Northeastern's master of science in corporate and organizational communication program, puts it, "Branding is what companies stand for. It's about their actions, their service, their shared values, and how they portray them to the world."

But let's dive a bit deeper. Have you ever considered that branding isn't exclusive to big-name companies? It's for everyone. Yes, even as an employee you are managing a personal brand and a visibility strategy! From the interns to the executive management team, each person carries a unique personal brand. Think of it as the stories we tell, the talents we showcase, and the legacies we hope to leave behind in the workplace and with our careers. Your personal brand is what your teammates say about you when you're not in the conference room or on Zoom, Microsoft Teams or Google Meet. Are you the unsung hero, consistently delivering without the spotlight, or are you the dynamic force everyone notices during meetings and team calls?

Your personal brand influences how your peers and management view you, and it shapes their feedback during reviews, appraisals, and possibly your promotion to the next position or increased bonuses. More importantly, it can impact your personal morale and the collective morale. Embracing, building, and making small pivots with your personal brand can be a game changer in Corporate America, making it a win-win for everyone. Even a pivot in another direction can give you a different vantage point about your personal brand and your career. Did you know that a pivot can mean a simple turn (i.e. going North East instead of North) or a complete change (i.e. going South instead of North) in the way in which one does something? My hope is that this chapter will help position you for whatever pivots you want to make with your career, ultimately putting more money in your pockets.

As mentioned previously, we typically think about branding for big companies and small businesses. My company, Mitchell Productions, works with small businesses and entrepreneurs on their marketing, branding, and visibility strategies, but something very interesting started to happen. After working with one client for a year on the marketing and branding of her side business, she pulled me to the side to share an unexpected impact. This client started implementing personal branding and visibilities strategies on her job, and she had been promoted twice! She attributed the promotions to her new focus on personal branding. She believed making the pivot to focus on her personal brand positioned her with the right visibility for the promotions.

Another client who works in the insurance field approached me with a similar "good news" story. After intentionally working on her personal branding and visibility strategies, she was recognized by her partnering insurance company and given higher commissions for her sales. This client also attributed this increased income to her small pivot to focus on branding strategies.

After hearing these testimonials, I had an epiphany. Personal branding can help your career goals in Corporate America. You might be asking, "How do I build and manage my personal brand so that I increase my morale, performance, and position myself for my next pivot?" That's what this chapter is all about! We will discuss a six-part framework that I will refer to as

The Platform Builder®.

But first...

In a rapidly evolving corporate landscape, mere skill acquisition isn't enough. What truly distinguishes an individual is how they curate and position their personal brand. For you, the reader and valuable employee, this is not merely about professional advancement; it's about crafting a legacy and destiny. *Positioned to Pivot* goes beyond generic advice. It's a tailored blueprint that empowers you to harness your unique strengths, passions, and aspirations. Why does this matter? Because in an age where roles evolve and industries transform, having a robust personal brand ensures you're not just adapting, but leading the change or pivot. It's about securing your place in the organization, not as a mere contributor but as an indispensable asset. This journey is about recognizing your value, amplifying your voice, and ensuring your hard work translates into tangible growth. Dive in, because this is about your morale, your career destiny, and your mark on the corporate world.

Are you ready to embark on this journey of self-discovery and owning your personal brand? Let's build your platform to showcase the asset that you are to your employer and raise the visibility of the work you are already doing!

No. 1 - Discover Your Unique Strengths

Every individual has a unique set of strengths and passions that sets them apart. It's time to uncover yours.

In the vast expanse of the corporate world, what makes you distinct, a cut above, and irreplaceable? It's a critical question, not just from a philosophical standpoint, but from a strategic one. To navigate the corporate ladder and stand out for that lateral or vertical promotion or the stellar review, one must start at the foundation: recognizing your unique strengths and passion.

The Intersection of Talent and Passion

Everyone has a set of talents—inherent or learned skills that set them apart. But talent alone isn't the endgame. It's when these talents intersect with personal passion that magic happens. Think of it this way: talents are what you're good at, but passions are what you're excited about. Merging the two can ignite a spark, leading to a better work-life balance, enhanced performance, and unmissable presence in the workplace.

Finding Your Strengths

Your strengths might be closer than they appear. Begin by reflecting on past projects, tasks, or roles where you not only excelled but also genuinely enjoyed the process. Think of things that you do effortlessly but other people struggle with. If introspection doesn't provide a clear picture, consider seeking feedback. Remember those late nights when you managed to crack a solution that no one else could? Or that presentation that had everyone talking? Well, your peers will remember. Peer feedback can be a mirror, reflecting qualities you might not even realize you possess.

Also look outside of the workplace. What comes natural to you? Are you the person in your family who always plans the big holiday meals, family reunions, or family trips? That shows your strength in event planning and project management.

For a more structured approach, consider strength-assessment tools or personality tests. Tools like StrengthsFinder (CliftonStrengths), the Myers-Briggs Type Indicator, Wiley's DiSC, Energy Leadership Index Assessment, Kolbe assessment and Fascinate test can offer detailed insights into your natural aptitudes and inclinations. But while these tools can guide you, always filter the results through your self-awareness and personal experiences.

Nurturing Your Passion

Unearthing your passion requires a different kind of digging. Think back to moments in your job that didn't feel like work, where hours felt like minutes. Was it when you were brainstorming creative concepts, analyzing data spreadsheets, or perhaps mentoring a colleague? These are the tasks that fuel your professional fire.

It's also important to realize that passion isn't static. It evolves. Something that energized you five years ago might not hold the same allure today. This is why regular self-reflection is important.

Why Does This Matter?

Here's why it matters. An employee who is aligned with their strengths and passions doesn't just meet targets; they redefine them. They bring innovation, enthusiasm, and a proactive mindset. Their work isn't just a checklist of tasks but a canvas of potential. Managers and leaders recognize this. They see the value in an employee who not only brings technical expertise but also genuine engagement to the table.

Moreover, when you operate from a place of strength and passion, challenges become opportunities for growth, and monotony transforms into a chance for innovation. Such an attitude is magnetic. It attracts attention, collaboration, and ultimately, recognition.

Taking Action

Now that you've identified these two pillars (strengths and passions), it's time for the fun part: showcasing them. Start by aligning your tasks and projects with your strengths. I recognize that this may not be possible in all roles and companies but make an attempt. Volunteer for initiatives that resonate with your passion. But remember, it's not about taking on more than you can handle; it's about strategically choosing tasks where you can shine the brightest based on your strengths and passions.

In meetings, discussions, or reviews, highlight results and approaches that stem from your unique strengths and passion. The key is to be genuine and authentic.

Building and managing a personal brand in the workplace isn't just about being visible. It's about being memorable for the right reasons. And the cornerstone of this journey is understanding and harnessing your unique strengths and passion. When you do, not only will better reviews and promotions be within reach, but you'll also find greater satisfaction and meaning in your career.

[RECAP] No. 1 - Discover Your Unique Strengths

Action Steps:

- Reflect on your accomplishments and challenges.
- Seek feedback from peers and mentors about your strengths.
- Document your key strengths and areas of passion.

* * *

No. 2 - Set Clear and Ambitious Goals

If discovering your strengths and passions is the foundation of your professional platform, setting clear and ambitious goals is the blueprint that will guide your career trajectory.

The theme song from the classic movie *Mahogany* starring Diana Ross was entitled, "Do You Know Where You're Going To?" That's the question on the table for you today.

In the realm of personal branding, it's not enough to be competent and passionate. One must be directionally focused, ensuring that each step, each project, and each effort aligns with your larger purpose.

The Power of Purposeful Direction

Purposeful direction often spells the difference between an employee who's great at their job and one poised for leadership. When you're clear about where you want to go, it not only impacts your performance but also how others perceive you. An employee with ambition and clear goals is seen as proactive, future-focused, and a valuable asset to any organization.

Crafting Your Goals

Begin by envisioning where you'd like to be in the next year, three years, or even five years. Consider roles you aspire to, skills you want to acquire, and the impact you aim to make. This can include lateral movement or vertical movement within your company.

Once you have a broad vision, it's time to break it down.

First, ensure your goals are S.M.A.R.T.:

1. **Specific:** Clearly define what you want to achieve.
2. **Measurable:** Determine how you'll track your progress.
3. **Achievable:** While ambition is key, realism ensures you're not setting yourself up for disappointment.
4. **Relevant:** Align your goals with your strengths, passions, and the organization's objectives.
5. **Time-bound:** Set deadlines to maintain momentum.

Next, categorize your goals. Some will be short-term (achievable in a year or less), while others will be long-term (taking multiple years). This differentiation helps prioritize your actions and allocate your time, attention, and energy effectively.

Syncing with Organizational Objectives

A pivotal step, often overlooked, is aligning personal ambitions with organizational goals. Why is this critical? Because when your growth trajectory benefits the company, it becomes a mutually beneficial relationship. It means you're not just seeking personal advancement but are genuinely invested in the company's success. This alignment is a powerful statement and one that management takes note of during reviews and promotion considerations.

Review and Adjust

Your goals aren't set in stone. As you progress in your career, as the company evolves, or as the industry landscape changes, it's essential to revisit and adjust your goals. Regular check-ins (monthly, quarterly, or at least biannually) ensure you remain on track and allow for timely pivots if necessary.

Communicate Your Goals

Having goals is one thing, but communicating them effectively is another. In discussions with your manager, a trusted mentor, or during team meetings, articulate not just what your goals are but also how they align with team or organizational objectives. It showcases foresight and initiative, qualities that are highly valued and help with your positioning.

Why Goal Setting Matters

When you understand what you are working toward, you are more likely to feel motivated and engaged. This clarity reduces confusion and helps focus your efforts effectively.

Achieving goals gives you as the employee and team member a sense of accomplishment. This boosts your self-esteem and confidence in your abilities. Regularly setting and achieving goals can create a positive cycle of growth and satisfaction.

In addition, when review time rolls around or when a higher position opens up, decision makers don't just evaluate past performance. They assess potential, dedication, and vision for the future. An employee with clear, ambitious goals that are communicated and aligned with the organization stands out. They present themselves as not just a contributor but a strategic player with a roadmap for future success.

This proactive approach not only accelerates your path to promotions but also imprints your unique personal brand and platform on the organization's fabric.

[RECAP] No. 2 - Set Clear and Ambitious Goals

Setting goals is like plotting points on a map, guiding you toward the career destiny you desire.

Action Steps:

- Define your short-term and long-term professional aspirations.
- Align your goals with organizational objectives.
- Regularly review and adjust your goals based on feedback and changing circumstances.

* * *

No. 3 - Express Your Brand Voice

In the modern workplace, characterized by diversity, emerging artificial intelligence, digital integration, and global impacts, merely having a personal brand isn't enough. The real magic lies in projecting it, making sure it's recognized, understood, and valued. But here's the challenge: How do you strike the balance between being assertive without coming off as overbearing? How do you ensure your brand voice is heard and not just part of the background noise?

Understanding Your Brand Voice

Before projecting your brand voice, take a moment to understand it deeply. Your brand voice isn't just about what you say; it's about how you say it. It's a mix of your input, perspectives, values, passions, strengths, and aspirations. It's how you approach challenges, collaborate with teams, and drive results. It embodies your professional communication skills.

As you intentionally use your voice as an employee, keep in mind the three components that make up communication:

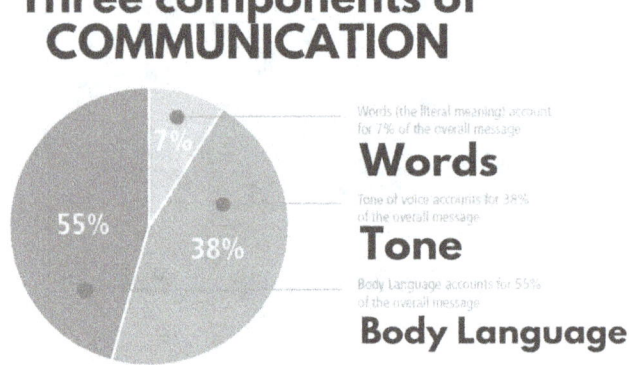

Three components of COMMUNICATION

7%
55%
38%

Words (the literal meaning) account for 7% of the overall message
Words

Tone of voice accounts for 38% of the overall message
Tone

Body Language accounts for 55% of the overall message
Body Language

Opportunities to Project Your Voice

In the workplace, there are a myriad of avenues to express your brand voice:

1. **Speaking Opportunities:** Volunteer for presentations, lead team meetings, or even offer to represent your department in inter-departmental sessions. These platforms allow your voice to be heard by a wider audience, establishing your authority and expertise. Here's the thing:

surveys typically indicate that between 72-75% of the population fears public speaking. So you rise to the top when you embrace public speaking to position you as a leader.

2. **Company Channels:** Contribute to the company's intranet, newsletters, or blog. Share insights, success stories, or even lessons from failures. Demonstrating thought leadership through written content can be a powerful brand-building tool and visibility strategy.

3. **Active Participation:** During meetings, offsites, team retreats, training classes or brainstorming sessions, engage actively. Pose questions, appear "on camera" for virtual meetings, offer solutions, and provide constructive feedback. Remember, it's not about speaking the most but about adding value.

4. **External Engagements:** Represent your organization in external forums, expos, conferences, or workshops. Being the face of your company not only enhances your personal brand but also demonstrates your commitment to your organization.

Authenticity Is Key

People can sense pretense. While it's crucial to be active, ensure every action, every word, resonates with genuine belief and intent. Authenticity builds trust, and trust amplifies your brand voice like nothing else.

Navigating Challenges

It's not always smooth sailing. You might encounter situations where your views are challenged or your approach is critiqued. These are not setbacks but opportunities. How you navigate disagreements, accept feedback, and adjust your strategies can significantly bolster your platform. Always remember, resilience and adaptability are as much a part of your brand voice as your successes.

Why Your Brand Voice Matters

In the symphony of the corporate world, every employee has a unique tune. The challenge and opportunity lie in ensuring it's heard and appreciated. By expressing your brand voice broadly, you not only underscore your value but also inspire others to find and project their unique voices. It's not just about personal elevation; it's about collectively elevating the workplace's vibrancy and innovation.

Furthermore, reviews and promotions are not just a retrospective look at performance but a gauge of future potential. By expressing your brand voice, you make a compelling case for both. You demonstrate a proactive mindset, leadership capabilities, and a commitment to personal and organizational growth. You position yourself not just as an individual contributor but as an influencer, a trendsetter.

When decision makers discuss promotions, they're more likely to favor someone whose contributions and values they're familiar with. In other words, if they know your song, they're more likely to give you the stage.

[RECAP] No. 3 - Express Your Brand Voice

Having a voice and sharing it in the workplace is vital. Don't shrink or hide but "take up space." Here's how to ensure your brand voice resonates:

Action Steps:

- Volunteer for speaking opportunities at company meetings or events.

- Contribute written thought leadership pieces to the company intranet or newsletter.
- Participate actively in team discussions and project collaborations, showcasing your unique insights.

* * *

No. 4 - Steward Your Development

Embarking on the journey of personal branding is a commitment, a pact you make with yourself. But unlike other commitments that demand rigid adherence, this one thrives on evolution, adaptability, and continuous growth. In the heart of this voyage lies the principle of stewardship. To steward your professional development is to **own it, nurture it,** and **guide it** with intentionality.

I heard someone say, "You can have the best manager in the world, but they cannot care more about your development than you do."

So let's start with a question: Why does stewardship, especially in the context of professional development, hold such significance? The answer lies in the distinction between passive learning and proactive growth. While the former waits for opportunities, the latter creates them.

Stewardship means taking charge, seeking out avenues for development, fostering a sense of belonging and ensuring every step aligns with your broader career vision.

Laying the Groundwork

Before you can steward your development, you must understand its current state. What skills do you possess? Where are the gaps? How do your strengths and areas of improvement align with industry and organizational demands? Answering these questions forms the basis of your development blueprint.

Seeking and Seizing Learning Opportunities

Once you have a clear picture of your current standing, pursue growth avenues. This could mean:

1. **Professional Courses and Certifications:** In our rapidly evolving world, staying updated with the latest industry trends and acquiring relevant certifications can offer a competitive edge.
2. **Workshops, Webinars, eLearnings and Seminars:** These are excellent platforms to not just gain knowledge but also to network and understand broader industry perspectives.
3. **Cross Training:** Cross-training (laterally or vertically) allows you to step into different roles and responsibilities, broadening your skill set. By actively seeking cross-training opportunities, you not only signal your commitment to growth but also position yourself as a versatile and invaluable asset to your team.

4. **Mentorship:** Identify individuals, within or outside your organization, who've treaded the path you aspire to walk. Their insights, guidance, and feedback can be invaluable.

Integrating Learning

Acquiring knowledge is one part of the puzzle; the real challenge is integration. How do you implement your learnings in real-world scenarios? Start by identifying projects or tasks that align with your newly acquired skills. Showcase your enhanced capabilities, and always be open to feedback. Remember, every implementation is also a learning opportunity.

Staying Updated

In the age of digital transformation and an evolving work environment, staying updated is not a luxury; it's a necessity. Look internally for information and updates put out by your company. Subscribe to industry journals, follow thought leaders on social and professional platforms, and engage in internal forums and discussions. Knowledge in today's world is as much about depth as it is about breadth.

Maintaining a Growth Journal

Document your learning journey. A growth journal can help you track courses completed, skills acquired, and milestones achieved. But more than just a log, it's a reflective tool. Review it periodically to understand patterns, identify areas of further exploration, and celebrate how far you've come. For some people, this may be an actual journal with pen and paper. For someone else, their growth journal might be a spreadsheet. Do what works for you.

Why Stewardship Matters?

The realm of personal branding in the workplace is intricate and multifaceted. While strengths, passions, goals, and brand voice form its pillars, continuous development is its lifeblood.

Stewarding this development isn't just about scaling the corporate ladder; it's about shaping the kind of professional you aspire to be. It's about recognizing the pivots and shifts you want to make.

When appraisal time rolls around or when promotions are on the table, a professional who's stewarded their development stands out. They showcase not just skills, but initiative. They demonstrate an investment in their growth, which translates to an investment in the organization's success and mission.

Managers and decision makers notice employees who don't just adapt to change but anticipate and drive it. Stewarding your professional development is a testament to this proactive, forward-thinking mindset.

[RECAP] No. 4 - Steward Your Development

Action Steps:

- Prioritize learning as a non-negotiable aspect of your career journey.
- Identify gaps in your skills and seek training or mentorship to fill them.
- Share and apply your acquired knowledge, becoming a beacon of expertise and inspiration for others.

No. 5 - Network Intentionally

The corporate world often mirrors a bustling city. Amid its skyscrapers of ambition and highways of opportunity, the currency that often holds the most value isn't just talent or hard work, but relationships. Networking, when done with intentionality, can be a catalyst to greater job satisfaction and career growth, opening doors you didn't even know existed.

The Essence of Intentional Networking

At the heart of intentional networking is purpose. It's not about just jumping on a virtual coffee break, collecting business cards, or adding LinkedIn connections haphazardly. It's about forging meaningful, mutual relationships. It's about understanding that every interaction holds potential—potential for collaboration, mentorship, or simply a fresh perspective.

Start Here:

1. **Know Your Why:** Before diving into networking, clarify your purpose. Are you seeking mentorship, looking for collaborators on a project, or simply wishing to broaden your knowledge of another department? Knowing your why will guide your how.
2. **Internal Networking:** Networking isn't always about reaching out externally. Your organization is a goldmine of expertise and experience. Engage in cross-departmental projects, attend companywide seminars, or simply strike up a conversation with someone from a different team. You'd be surprised at the insights you can gain.
3. **Industry Events:** Attend workshops, conferences, and seminars related to your field. Not only do these events offer knowledge, but they also present a chance to connect with like-minded professionals.

The Art of Authentic Engagement

1. **Listen Actively:** Networking isn't just about speaking; it's as much about listening. Understand the perspectives and challenges of others. It fosters deeper connections and showcases your genuine interest.
2. **Offer Value:** Networking is a two-way street. While seeking insights or opportunities, always consider what you bring to the table. It could be your expertise, a unique skill, or even a different viewpoint.
3. **Follow Up:** Met someone interesting at a company "all hands" meeting, team-building activity, or company holiday party? Send a follow-up email or a LinkedIn request and message. Mention something about the person or something

the two of you discussed. *This will be a great way to jog your memory later!* Also express interest in staying connected.

Nurturing Your Network

Networking doesn't end at the first interaction. It's about nurturing these relationships over time. Share articles or research you believe might interest them. Congratulate them on their achievements. Or simply check in once in a while to see how they're doing. Remember, genuine relationships are built on mutual respect and interest.

Digital Networking

In our digital age, networking isn't restricted to physical events. Platforms like company intranet sites, company chat systems, Slack, LinkedIn, et cetera, offer vast opportunities. Engage in discussions, share your insights, and connect.

Why Intentional Networking Matters

Here's the thing: When it comes to promotions or appraisals, it's not just about how well you do your job, but how well others *know* you do your job. Networking can enable your achievements, capabilities, and potential to be recognized more broadly.

Additionally, the relationships you build can provide invaluable feedback, helping you refine your skills and approach. They can offer mentorship, guiding your career trajectory, or they can even present opportunities, perhaps a project or role you hadn't even considered.

In the grand tapestry of building a personal brand and platform in the workplace, networking threads it all together. It's about recognizing and leveraging the collective power of professional relationships.

As you network with intentionality, authenticity, and purpose, you'll find not only doors of opportunities swinging open but also a richer, more holistic professional journey unfolding.

[RECAP] No. 5 - Network Intentionally

Action Steps:

- Engage in company events and team-building activities.
- Connect on company intranet sites.
- Attend industry conferences, workshops, webinars, and seminars.
- Build and nurture genuine relationships both within and outside the organization.

No. 6 - Amplify Your Achievements

Have you been to a music concert at any point in life or seen one on TV?

A stage or platform at a music concert serves three important purposes:

1. **Visibility:** The primary purpose of a stage or platform is to elevate the performers, making them visible to the audience. Without a raised platform, it would be challenging for attendees, especially those farther back, to see the musicians and performers.
2. **Acoustics:** Stages or platforms are often designed to enhance the acoustics of a performance. The elevation helps project or amplify sound more effectively across the audience.
3. **Focus and Attention:** A stage acts as a focal point, directing the audience's attention toward the performers. It helps create a central point of interest, which is essential for maintaining the audience's engagement throughout the concert.

In the concert of corporate life, where everyone plays their unique tunes, how do you ensure your melody doesn't get lost in the music? The key lies not just in performing exceptionally but in amplifying your achievements. It's about celebrating your milestones, not as a form of boastfulness, but as a testament to your dedication, hard work, and contribution.

The Balance of Humility and Recognition

Many of us have been taught that humility is a virtue—and it undoubtedly is. But there's a fine line between humility and self-sabotage. While it's essential to be grounded, it's equally crucial to ensure that your work and contributions are recognized.

Why Amplification Matters...

In large organizations where a myriad of projects run simultaneously and teams collaborate across geographies, it's easy for individual accomplishments to get overshadowed or drowned out in the noise. Amplifying your achievements ensures:

1. **Visibility:** Your superiors and peers recognize your contribution.
2. **Opportunities:** With recognition comes the chance for further collaboration, projects, or even promotions.
3. **Personal Branding:** Shining a spotlight on your achievements reinforces your personal brand, showcasing you as someone who drives results and adds value.

Strategies for Visibility

1. **Document Religiously:** Keep a real-time record of your achievements (i.e., a brag book). Whether it's a project you've completed ahead of time, a solution you've innovated, or positive feedback from a client, jot it down. This record isn't just for communicating achievements to your supervisor or leadership team but also a personal reminder of your growth and capabilities.
2. **Communicate Strategically:** During team meetings or one-on-one sessions with your manager, weave in your achievements. For instance, when discussing a new project, you can reference a similar past assignment and its successful outcome.

3. **Leverage Platforms:** Utilize platforms like the company intranet, newsletters, or even LinkedIn to share milestones. It could be a case study, a project snapshot, or even a testimonial.

4. **Seek Advocates or Sponsors:** Build relationships with peers and superiors who recognize and value your contribution. They can amplify your achievements in forums you might not have access to.

5. **Mentor and Guide Others:** Share your experiences and knowledge with junior team members. When you help others succeed, your achievements get naturally highlighted.

6. **Engage in Reviews:** During performance reviews, leverage your documented achievements. It offers a concrete, data-backed representation of your contributions. We literally can't remember all of the things we have accomplished over a year, that's where the brag book comes in handy.

Managing Challenges

It's not always a smooth ride. You might face questions, even skepticism, especially if you're breaking traditional norms of humility. Here's a piece of advice: Always root your actions in facts and genuine intent. It's not about projecting superiority but about factual representation.

When Faced with Challenges or Questions:

1. **Stay Calm:** Defensive reactions can dilute your message.
2. **Use Data:** Back your achievements with data, feedback, or tangible results.

3. **Seek Feedback**: If someone feels your amplification of your achievements is excessive, seek feedback. Understand their perspective and adjust your approach if necessary.

Amplifying achievements in the workplace isn't just a strategy; it's a necessity in today's competitive environment. As you build your platform and manage your personal brand, remember that your achievements are its cornerstone.

By amplifying them with authenticity and strategy, you not only pave the way for promotions and better reviews but also inspire others to reach for excellence. After all, in the journey of professional growth, it's not just about reaching the summit but illuminating the path for others to follow.

[RECAP] No. 6 - Amplify Your Achievements

Celebrating your successes is not bragging; it's a testament to your dedication and work contributions.

Action Steps:

- Document your milestones, achievements, and contributions.
- Share your success stories during performance reviews and other times.
- Mentor and guide others, using your experiences as instructive anecdotes.

In Closing...

In the vibrant tapestry of the corporate world, your unique thread—your personal brand—must weave its distinct pattern. This will help position you to pivot into the next role, project, or promotion. The six-part framework we've journeyed through is more than just a strategy; it's a clarion call to introspection, growth, and purposeful action.

From diving deep into your strengths and passions, setting the compass of your goals, expressing your authentic voice, stewarding your professional development, forging genuine connections, to celebrating your achievements and work contributions, each step is a layer in building your professional identity and platform. But, guess what? Beyond strategies and steps, it's about recognizing your worth, owning your narrative, and inspiring others with your professional journey.

As you embark on this building project, remember, it's not just about the accolades or the promotions; it's about your quality of work life, your morale, the lives you touch, and the change you champion.

Embrace The Platform Builder® framework, not just as an architectural guide but as a commitment to yourself, to your dreams, and to the indelible mark you're destined to leave in the world.

Finally, I leave you with The Platform Builder® checklist!

1. Discover your unique strengths.

[ ] Reflect on past roles or tasks where you excelled and felt genuine enjoyment.
[ ] Seek feedback from peers about your standout qualities.
[ ] Explore strength-assessment tools like StrengthsFinder or the Myers-Briggs Type Indicator.
[ ] Regularly set aside time for self-reflection to stay in touch with evolving passions.

2. Set clear and ambitious goals.

[ ] Visualize your career path for the next one, three, and five years.
[ ] Break down your vision into S.M.A.R.T. goals.
[ ] Align personal goals with organizational objectives.
[ ] Regularly revisit and adjust goals based on changing circumstances and growth.

3. Express your brand voice.

[ ] Identify speaking opportunities within the organization.
[ ] Contribute to company channels, such as the intranet or newsletters.
[ ] Actively participate in team meetings and brainstorming sessions.
[ ] Represent the organization in external forums and events.
[ ] Engage authentically and maintain consistent communication with peers and superiors.

4. Steward your professional development.

[ ] Assess current skills and identify gaps.
[ ] Seek out professional courses, certifications, workshops, and seminars.
[ ] Engage in mentorship opportunities.
[ ] Apply new learnings in real-world scenarios.
[ ] Stay updated with industry trends through journals, thought leaders, and forums.
[ ] Maintain a growth journal to track and reflect on progress.

5. Network intentionally.

[ ] Clarify the purpose of your networking efforts.

[ ] Engage in internal networking within the organization.
[ ] Attend industry-related events and conferences.
[ ] Engage authentically, listen actively, and provide value in interactions.
[ ] Follow up after meaningful conversations.
[ ] Foster and nurture relationships over time, ensuring mutual growth.

6. Amplify your achievements.

[ ] Regularly document your achievements, big or small in a brag book.
[ ] Strategically communicate milestones in relevant forums.
[ ] Leverage organizational platforms to share success stories.
[ ] Build relationships with advocates who recognize your contributions.
[ ] Share knowledge, and mentor other team members.
[ ] Engage actively in performance reviews, using your documented achievements as evidence of contribution.

Meet the Author | Sharvette Mitchell

Sharvette Mitchell, founder of Mitchell Productions, is more than a business leader and marketing consultant. She's THE PLATFORM BUILDER. Her vision, ingenuity, and extensive twenty-five-year background in corporate America at Capital One Bank, coupled with a Bachelor of Science in marketing from Virginia Commonwealth University, have crystallized her reputation as an authority in the marketing and branding landscape.

Sharvette's unique approach, encapsulated in her trademarked framework THE PLATFORM BUILDER, has become a beacon for small businesses seeking to amplify their brand. By honing their visibility, marketing, and branding strategies, she has enabled numerous businesses to generate more revenue, achieve growth, and establish increased brand recognition.

Her one-on-one consulting, innovative group coaching programs, engaging speaking/training, and live conferences/summits have been applauded for their effectiveness and creativity. As a marketing consultant, her insight into consumer behavior and online market trends has made her an indispensable asset for growing businesses aiming to elevate their brand presence in the competitive market.

The Platform Builder

Sharvette's acclaim extends to being featured in prestigious publications such as *Yahoo! Finance, AARP, Huffington Post, Hope for Women* magazine, *CBNation,* and *Sista Sense* magazine, where her thoughts on marketing and branding are often sought. Her appearances on CBS 6 *Monday Motivation,* CBS 6 *Virginia This Morning,* The CW Network, and Comcast Cable showcase her as a thought leader.

Her certifications as a Women-Owned Small Business (WOSB) with the U.S. Small Business Administration, Small, Women- and Minority-owned Businesses (SWaM) by the Virginia Department of Small Business and Supplier Diversity and MBE certification with the National Minority Supplier Development Council (NMSDC) demonstrate her commitment to inclusivity in the business landscape. Moreover, as an International Coaching Federation (ICF) Professional Certified Leadership Coach, Sharvette embodies a blend of coaching and influential leadership.

Since 2008, *The Sharvette Mitchell Radio Show,* with more than 730+ episodes, has been a platform for marketing insights, professional development, powerful conversations, and interviews, resonating with listeners and viewers across multiple audio and live-streaming platforms. Sharvette is a past recipient of the *ACHI Magazine*'s Radio Personality of the Year Award.

A prolific visionary author, Sharvette is behind five other impactful book collaborations, including *PROPEL, POUR, PURSUE, PEARLS,* and *Prepare for PURPOSE.* These works further illustrate her passion for guiding others to pursue their dreams and document their transformational stories or intellectual property.

Her previous role on the board of directors of James River Writers and current volunteer role with International Christian Ministries, Inc. attests to her contributions to the community and her peers.

Whether guiding a small business to marketing success, delivering powerful professional development training, or redefining a brand's identity, Sharvette's strategic mind and marketing expertise stand as a testament to what can be achieved with strategy, consistency, and leadership.

Learn more at www.Mitchell-Productions.com.

About Mitchell Productions

Mitchell Productions, LLC, Women-Owned Small Business (WOSB), Virginia certified Small, Woman- and Minority-Owned Business (SWaM) and National Minority Supplier Development Council (NMSDC) certified, is a marketing and professional development firm, led by Sharvette Mitchell, supporting entrepreneurs, small businesses as well as government clients and corporate clients.